I0021690

ARK ECOSYSTEM

POINT. CLICK. BLOCKCHAIN.

2016-2017-2018-2019

A CONCISE ARK ECOSYSTEM HISTORY BOOK

ARK Ecosystem—Point. Click. Blockchain.

by Christopher P. Thompson

Book authored by Christopher P. Thompson

Book design by C. Ellis

ISBN: 9781699908884

ARK ECOSYSTEM

POINT. CLICK. BLOCKCHAIN.

2016-2017-2018-2019

A CONCISE ARK ECOSYSTEM HISTORY BOOK

CHRISTOPHER P. THOMPSON

DELEGATE SPECIAL MENTIONS

During the time it took to write this book, several delegates generously donated to the author. Each delegate below has added value to the ARK Ecosystem in a diverse number of ways:

jarunik (donated 300 ARK)

He is a delegate with deep technical and economics understanding. In May 2017, he was one of the initial people to be elected as an ACF board member. He has forged over 150,000 mainnet ARK blockchain blocks.

cams_yellow_jacket (donated 200 ARK)

They have contributed to the ARK Ecosystem by producing informative videos including the 'ARK at Consensus 2018' video (published on 24th May 2018). They have forged over 70,000 mainnet ARK blockchain blocks.

drakeler (donated 100 ARK)

He has enthusiastically answered questions from the community and contributed to ongoing testing of the ARK Desktop and Mobile Wallets. He has forged over 15,000 mainnet ARK blockchain blocks.

civseed (donated 59.38318044 ARK)

He runs the http://ark.party/ website. He has forged over 55,000 mainnet ARK blockchain blocks.

As well as the above, over 600 ARK were donated from unknown ARK Crew members, delegates or community members.

If you appreciate the work that went into this publication, feel free to support the author by donating to **AXm3fJ5JZ3jV8btqvMciuqAQN1JDeG4hts**

CONTENTS

INTRODUCTION

Since the inception of Bitcoin, thousands of cryptocurrencies or decentralised blockchains have been launched. Most ventures into the blockchain space have not gone according to plan as their founders would have hoped. Nevertheless, there are hundreds of blockchain projects which are succeeding.

This book covers the concise history of the ARK Ecosystem, a decentralised, globally accessible and secure ecosystem to empower everyone, regardless of their aim or technical background, to quickly and easily leverage blockchain technology.

Since September 2016, a growing ARK Crew and community have collaborated to create a resilient, efficient and secure decentralised network. What follows is a list of major accomplishments:

- ARK Ecosystem Token Exchange Campaign occurred (NOV/DEC 2016)
- Mainnet ARK blockchain launched (MARCH 2017)
- ARK integrated into Ledger Hardware Wallet devices (SEPTEMBER 2017)
- ARK registered as a SCIC in France (NOVEMBER 2017)
- ARK Mobile Wallet released (DECEMBER 2017)
- All time 2018 high ARK price recorded (JANUARY 2018)
- ARK Crew attended Consensus 2018 in New York City (MAY 2018)
- Mainnet ARK blockchain migrated to ARK Core V2 (DECEMBER 2018)
- ARK V2 Whitepaper published (APRIL 2019)
- ARK V2 Deployer (GUI) released (MAY 2019)
- ARK V2 official website went live for users and developers (JULY 2019)

INTRODUCTION

To be specific, this book covers a concise chronological series of events from the 11th September 2016 to the 9th July 2019. During this time, the ARK Ecosystem attracted growing interest from inside and outside the blockchain technology space.

You may have bought this book because the ARK Ecosystem is your favourite cryptographic blockchain project. Alternatively, you may be keen to find out how it all began. I have presented the information henceforth without going into too much technical discussion. If you would like to investigate further, I recommend that you read material currently available at https://ark.io or study the official ARK Ecosystem Whitepaper.

If you choose to purchase a certain amount of ARK, please do not buy more than you can afford to lose.

Enjoy the book :D

WHAT IS THE ARK ECOSYSTEM?

By optimising proven aspects of blockchain technology, and learning how it has fallen short over the preceding years, an initial team of passionate blockchain enthusiasts embarked on a voyage to create a more resilient, secure and efficient decentralised network. The ARK Ecosystem can be described as follows:

- It is a collection of interoperable blockchains that can communicate with each other (SmartBridge Technology) or remain isolated. The mainnet ARK blockchain is the hub of the network.
- It is a method by which people are free to use the native ARK cryptocurrency to pay for/sell goods or services. The ARK token serves as the main medium of exchange used to pay for delegate services, customised plugins, decentralised applications and so on. ARK is also a store of value.
- It is an ideal environment in which developers can prepare, customise and deploy blockchains in minutes by using the ARK Deployer. Developers can utilise an array of tools, programming languages and community expertise to develop, test and release customised plug-ins and applications.

Since its inception, the ARK Ecosystem has grown from strength to strength in terms of community developer participation and the size of its community. The long term goal is to provide the world with a highly adaptable, scalable and user friendly ecosystem. The ARK Crew is committed to see the ARK Ecosystem as the natural choice for creating disruptive, world-changing and innovative decentralised applications. It is officially described as:

> **"ARK empowers everyone, regardless of their aim or technical background, to quickly and easily leverage blockchain technology. We provide the tools and resources that enable individuals, developers and startups to apply blockchain technology as a foundation for their own projects, applications and ideas."**

WHY USE THE ARK ECOSYSTEM?

There are numerous ways in which decentralised networks are more favourable than centralised systems. What follows are some advantages that blockchain technology brings to the table:

- It can be used on a global scale without external permission being granted.
- No third parties need to be trusted to verify transactions or validate transfers of data from one entity to another.
- No malicious actors can falsify or remove data (it is immutable).
- It has no central point of failure (negligible downtime periods).
- It is free from government censorship or other third party interference.
- Delegates are rewarded the native ARK token for securing the network.
- Blocks add to the mainnet ARK blockchain every 8 seconds (highly efficient).
- It does not rely on one single blockchain. The ARK Deployer can be used to create custom ARK based blockchains (bridgechains) that help reduce the bloat experienced by the mainnet ARK blockchain (it is highly scalable).

CORE ARK ECOSYSTEM VALUES

To help steer the ARK Ecosystem through the rough seas of blockchain technology, six core values are proudly presented on the official website https://ark.io and other relevant documentation. They are:

1. **SIMPLICITY**: all aspects of the ecosystem are made as simple as possible in order for everyone to easily leverage the technology. End users are free to use the simple, clean and user friendly wallet client applications. Developers have the ability to create useful applications by utilising an array of easy to use tools and programming languages.

2. **SECURITY**: simply put, ARK nodes secure the decentralisation of the network and 51 delegates (chosen by ARK token holders) each forge 2 ARK per block via the delegated proof of stake (DPoS) consensus algorithm.

3. **SPEED**: the mainnet ARK blockchain is fast and efficient. In turn, 51 active delegates (within an approximate 408 second round) each forge 2 ARK every eight seconds or so (top 51 delegates can then change in the next round).

4. **SCALABILITY**: the ARK Ecosystem does not consist of one blockchain. The mainnet ARK blockchain can interoperate with an unlimited number of bridgechains. This allows the whole ecosystem to scale exponentially without slowing down transactions or other processes.

5. **SOVEREIGNTY**: the ability for individuals, businesses or other entities to create bespoke bridgechains without being bound to external rules. It is possible to create systems independent from the mainnet ARK blockchain.

6. **SUPPORT**: the ARK Ecosystem consists of skilled core developers, delegates and community developers who are able to support external entities by offering solutions or guiding them through technical processes.

SPECIFICATION

At the time of publication of this book, the mainnet ARK blockchain specification is:

Unit of Account:	ARK
Smallest Unit of Account:	1 ARKtoshi = 0.00000001 ARK
Time of Announcement:	15th October 2016 at 18:09:25 UTC
ARK Core V1 Launch Time:	21st March 2017 at 19:00 UTC
ARK Core V2 Launch Time:	3rd December 2018 at 16:00 UTC
Timestamping Algorithm:	Delegated Proof of Stake
Number of Active Delegates:	51
ARK Core Codebase:	TypeScript (formerly JavaScript)
Initial Coins:	125,000,000 ARK
Total Coins:	No limit (inflation tends to zero)
Block Reward:	2 ARK
Block Time:	8 seconds
Block Reward Halving:	None
Transaction Fees:	Dynamic Fees
Token Exchange Campaign:	Yes

MILESTONE TIMELINE

11th September 2016 —Official Slack channel and Facebook page created
12th September 2016 —Official ARK Ecosystem Twitter account was created
11th October 2016 —Official ARK Ecosystem Subreddit created
15th October 2016 —Official PRE-ANN on Bitcointalk created
25th October 2016 —Official announcement of Ark Ecosystem
7th November 2016 —ARK Token Exchange Campaign began
12th November 2016 —ARK source code released on Github
8th December 2016 —First publicly available ARK Testnet launched
11th December 2016 —ARK Token Exchange Campaign ended

2017

3rd March 2017 —Mainnet ARK blockchain launch date announced
21st March 2017 —Desktop wallet version 1.0.1 released
21st March 2017 —ARK mainnet blockchain launched at 19:00 UTC
21st March 2017 —Bittrex exchange initiated ARK trading
22nd March 2017 —Cryptopia exchange initiated ARK trading
28th March 2017 —Delegate forging rewards began
28th March 2017 —Desktop wallet version 1.0.2 released
28th March 2017 —Desktop wallet version 1.1.0 released
24th April 2017 —LiteBit.eu exchange initiated ARK trading
27th April 2017 —Desktop wallet version 1.2.0 released
10th May 2017 —Desktop wallet version 1.2.1 released
13th May 2017 —Desktop wallet version 1.2.2 released
20th May 2017 —ARK Community Fund (ACF) went live
1st June 2017 —Lúcio Rubens joined the ARK Crew
7th June 2017 —ARK price surpassed US$1 for the first time
7th August 2017 —Desktop wallet version 1.3.0 released

MILESTONE TIMELINE

16th August 2017	—Desktop wallet version 1.3.1 released
1st September 2017	—ARK integration into Ledger occurred
1st September 2017	—Oleg Shcherbyna joined the ARK Crew
4th September 2017	—Desktop wallet version 1.3.2 released
2nd October 2017	—Cryptomate UK exchange initiated ARK trading
9th October 2017	—Desktop wallet version 1.4.0 released
10th October 2017	—Desktop wallet version 1.4.1 released
24th October 2017	—Upbit exchange initiated ARK trading
1st November 2017	—Binance exchange initiated ARK trading
3rd November 2017	—Juan A Martin joined the ARK Crew
11th November 2017	—Bit-Z exchange initiated ARK trading
14th November 2017	—Alex Barnsley joined the ARK Crew
18th November 2017	—Desktop wallet version 1.4.2 released
21st November 2017	—Desktop wallet version 1.4.3 released
21st November 2017	—ARK registered in France as a SCIC
18th December 2017	—Kristjan Košič joined the ARK Crew
20th December 2017	—OKEX exchange initiated ARK trading
21st December 2017	—All time high 2017 ARK price recorded at US$9.11
27th December 2017	—Mobile wallet version 1.0.0 released

2018

9th January 2018	—Desktop wallet version 1.5.0 released
9th January 2018	—All time high 2018 ARK price recorded at US$10.91
20th January 2018	—ARK Deployer V1 officially released
25th January 2018	—Desktop wallet version 1.5.1 released
14th February 2018	—Jeremy Epstein joined the ARK Crew
13th March 2018	—Livecoin exchange initiated ARK trading

MILESTONE TIMELINE

26th March 2018	—GODEX exchange initiated ARK trading
4th April 2018	—Simon Downey joined the ARK Crew
1st May 2018	—Adrian Kerchev joined the ARK Crew
14th-16th May 2018	—Consensus 2018 in New York City occurred
21st May 2018	—Exrates.me exchange initiated ARK trading
25th May 2018	—ARK became available on Changelly
31st May 2018	—Ark Mobile wallet for iOS released
14th June 2018	—ARK Core V2 Devnet was released
27th June 2018	—Desktop wallet version 1.6.0 released
20th July 2018	—Desktop wallet version 1.6.1 released
31st July 2018	—Gerard Blezer joined the ARK Crew
1st August 2018	—Carlye Wicklund joined the ARK Crew
13th August 2018	—Justin Renken joined the ARK Crew
14th August 2018	—Mario Vega joined the ARK Crew
15th August 2018	—New ARK Core V2 Devnet was released
20th August 2018	—Erwann Gentric joined the ARK Crew
3rd September 2018	—Joshua Noack joined the ARK Crew
6th September 2018	—Major League Hacking partnership announced
13th September 2018	—ARK Mobile wallet version 1.2 released
19th-20th September 2018	—Consensus 2018 in Singapore occurred
24th September 2018	—Vasil Dimov joined the ARK Crew
1st November 2018	—ARK V2 Testathon began
8th November 2018	—ARK V2 Testathon ended
28th November 2018	—ARK Core V2 migration on mainnet began
3rd December 2018	—Mainnet blockchain switched to ARK Core V2
3rd December 2018	—Desktop wallet version 2.0.0 released
4th December 2018	—ARK Core V2 migration on mainnet complete

MILESTONE TIMELINE

5th December 2018 —ARK Mobile Wallet version 1.3.1 released for Android
8th December 2018 —ARK Mobile Wallet version 1.3.1 released for iOS
11th December 2018 —Sam Harper-Pittam joined the ARK Crew
14th December 2018 —ARK Desktop Wallet version 2.1.0 released
21st December 2018 —ARK Desktop Wallet version 2.1.1 released

2019

17th January 2019 —ARK Desktop wallet version 2.2.0 released
30th January 2019 —ARK Desktop wallet version 2.2.1 released
8th February 2019 —ARK Mobile wallet version 1.4.0 released
20th February 2019 —ARK integrated into SpendApp
14th March 2019 —ARK Desktop wallet version 2.3.0 released
18th March 2019 —ARK Deployer version 2 (CLI) released
22nd March 2019 —ARK Desktop wallet version 2.3.1 released
25th March 2019 —ARK Desktop wallet version 2.3.2 released
4th April 2019 —Michel Kraaijeveld joined the ARK Crew
5th April 2019 —Whitepaper V2 published
13th-15th May 2019 —Consensus 2019 in New York City occurred
21st May 2019 —ARK Desktop wallet version 2.4.0 released
28th May 2019 —ARK Deployer V2 (GUI) released
10th June 2019 —DOBI exchange
12th June 2019 —ARK Desktop wallet version 2.4.1 released
14th June 2019 —ARK Mobile wallet version 1.4.4 released
26th June 2019 —ARK Desktop wallet version 2.5.0 released
9th July 2019 —Official ark.io website V2 went live

BLOCKCHAIN

Blockchain technology was introduced to the world when Satoshi Nakamoto published the Bitcoin whitepaper in October 2008. Since that time, the concept of blockchain has grown, advanced and proliferated. It has the potential to impact society in innumerable realised and unforeseen ways.

A blockchain is usually described as a distributed public ledger of all transactions (contained within blocks) ever executed since the first block. Unlike relying on third parties to record financial transactions, trust is automatically enforced by decentralised code protocol. A dynamic group of 51 active delegates are collectively responsible for validating transactions, which are then grouped together in a block every eight seconds. Blocks are added to the blockchain in such a manner that each block contains the hash of the prior one. It is therefore utterly resistant to modification. Consequently, the problem of double-spending is solved.

Unlike Bitcoin and other blockchains, the ARK Ecosystem consists of the mainnet ARK blockchain and a spiderweb of an unlimited number of bridgechains. It is possible for developers to prepare, customise and deploy bespoke blockchains by using the innovative ARK Deployer. These bridgechains (ARK based blockchains) can then interoperate with the mainnet ARK blockchain (remains unbloated and efficient) by using a section of the ARK Core codebase known as the VendorField. The VendorField is a direct messaging system that allows blockchains to send data/ functions back and forth with each other. This technology is called SmartBridge.

On the 21st March 2017, after months of development and testing, the mainnet ARK blockchain successfully launched with the creation of the genesis block. Block number one generated 125 million ARK (see immediately below).

Block #1 (Reward 125,000,000 ARK) March 21st 2017 at 19:00 UTC

BLOCKCHAIN

To browse and investigate activity on the mainnet ARK blockchain, the official ARK Explorer at https://explorer.ark.io/ is freely available. It is an online fundamental tool, designed from scratch using the Vue.js and TailwindCSS frameworks, providing real-time data such as:

- All the latest transactions processed after being added to blocks.
- Current balances of all wallet addresses.
- All the latest blocks timestamped.
- The ability to monitor active delegates and standby delegates.
- The ability to check the top wallet addresses.

DELEGATED PROOF OF STAKE

As an alternative to the proof of work consensus mechanism used to secure the decentralisation of the Bitcoin network, the mainnet ARK blockchain is secured by a modified version of delegated proof of stake. Delegated proof of stake, or DPoS for short, is the method by which transactions on the blockchain are validated, without third party oversight, by delegates before being added to blocks. It was invented by Daniel Larimer (the founder of BitShares, Steemit and EOS) as an alternative to both proof of work (high energy cost) and proof of stake (less representative).

Besides being relatively energy efficient, DPoS is a democratic mechanism that uses voting to decide which delegates (node administrators) run and secure the mainnet ARK blockchain. ARK token holders are able to vote for which delegates they deem to be trustworthy and those which add value to the ecosystem. If a delegate begins to act dishonestly or maliciously, ARK token holders can decide, at any time, to vote for another or none at all. What follows are the specifics of the voting process:

- Each wallet address can be used to vote for a delegate by sending a special transaction from within either the ARK Desktop or ARK Mobile Wallets.
- Once a wallet address has assigned the vote, the number of ARK held in that wallet address adds to the cumulative weight of the voted delegate.
- The total of all voting weight from all wallet addresses determines the rank of the delegate. Only the top 51 delegates can forge new ARK tokens (new delegates can enter the top 51 after each approximate 408 seconds round).

Delegated proof of stake allows the mainnet ARK blockchain to process blocks at a relatively high speed of eight seconds. It is faster than the Bitcoin blockchain that adds blocks every ten minutes or so. Other cryptographic blockchains that use delegated proof of stake include Lisk, Steem, EOS and BitShares.

FORGING REWARDS

As an incentive for running safe nodes and securing the mainnet ARK blockchain, all active delegates (within an approximate 408 seconds round) each, in turn, receive 2 ARK by forging the next block. This process then repeats for the next top 51 delegates chosen by the ARK token holders. Additionally, the delegate who forges a block will also receive all transaction fees that were processed during that same block. Delegates ranked below position 51 (relay nodes) help to secure the network, but do not receive forging rewards.

Initially, after the first block generated 125 million ARK, no forging rewards existed until block number 75,600 (see below). All transaction fees generated before this block were evenly split between the 'Magnificient Seven'. They were dafty, sidzero, michaelthecryptoguy, ghostfaceuk, bcboilermaker, jamiec79 and toons.

Block #75,600 (Reward 2 ARK) March 28th 2017 at 22:20:16 UTC

"Today officially marked the beginning of Delegate Forging Rewards and our hard working delegates will now be rewarded for running the network nodes that power the ARK. The initiation of rewards was an exciting time for our delegates and we can't wait to see how the 51 forging positions shake out."

ARK CORE

ARK Core is the backbone of the whole ARK Ecosystem. It is described as a lightweight, but powerful, codebase authored in the TypeScript programming language. Delegates or relay nodes must install, configure and monitor it as the means to operate a secure, efficient and resilient ecosystem.

Originally, the ARK Developers adopted the codebase of a previously launched blockchain called Lisk. It was subsequently highly modified and heavily optimised for the needs of ARK users. ARK Core V1 was released a few hours before the launch of the mainnet ARK blockchain on the 21st March 2017.

In November 2017, after much thought and deliberation, a decision was made to overhaul the legacy Lisk codebase. It had become too restrictive in terms of what the ARK Crew had planned to achieve according to set roadmap goals.

Following months of development, the mainnet ARK blockchain successfully migrated to ARK Core V2 (built from scratch) in December 2018.

Since the migration to ARK Core V2, several updates to the core codebase have been released during 2019:

- On the 11th February 2019, ARK Core version 2.1 was released. It primarily changed the codebase from JavaScript to TypeScript.
- On the 11th March 2019, ARK Core version 2.2 made the process of installing and managing ARK nodes easier.
- On the 23rd April 2019, ARK Core version 2.3 streamlined the process of developing the codebase. It increased the VendorField from 64 to 255 bytes.
- On the 12th June 2019, ARK Core version 2.4 improved the way in which ARK nodes interact with each other (better performance and more resilient).

WALLETS

Continuously improved to serve the needs the ARK community, ARK wallets are multi-functional applications rigorously tested and developed with user friendliness, simplicity, performance and security in mind. Both the ARK Desktop Wallet and Mobile Wallet have been developed in an open source environment by a celebrated collaborative effort between ARK Developers and community developers. They are secure ways to transact, and store, the native ARK cryptocurrency.

https://github.com/ArkEcosystem/desktop-wallet
https://github.com/ArkEcosystem/mobile-wallet

- The ARK Desktop Wallet is a lite client, written from scratch using VueJS and TailwindCSS, built for the Windows, Mac and Linux operating systems. It is compatible with Ledger devices such as the Ledger Nano S. It also connects to fully synchronised network peers removing the need to download the full blockchain.
- The ARK Mobile Wallet is a hybrid application useful for transacting ARK or voting for delegates on the go. It is available for Android and iOS devices.

CRYPTOCURRENCY EXCHANGES

Since the launch of the mainnet ARK blockchain, third party exchanges have made it possible for their users to trade the native ARK cryptocurrency. They are trading platforms on which people are free to buy or sell ARK, besides hundreds of other coins and tokens, at the going market rate. They also collectively determine the fiat price of each ARK token and the overall ARK market capitalisation.

What follows is a table of almost all exchanges which have enabled ARK trading:

Date Trading Initiated	Exchange	Trading Against	Status
21st March 2017	Bittrex	BTC	OPEN
22nd March 2017	Cryptopia		CLOSED
24th April 2017	LiteBit.eu		OPEN
9th June 2017	COSS	BTC, ETH, USD, USDT	OPEN
27th September 2017	BuyUcoin	INR	OPEN
2nd October 2017	Cryptomate	GBP	OPEN
24th October 2017	Upbit	BTC, KRW	OPEN
1st November 2017	Binance	BTC, ETH	OPEN
11th November 2017	Bit-Z	BTC	OPEN
20th December 2017	OKEX	BTC, ETH, USDT	OPEN
13th March 2018	Livecoin	BTC	OPEN
26th March 2018	GODEX		OPEN
15th May 2018	SimpleSwap		OPEN
21st May 2018	Exrates	BTC, ETH	OPEN
25th July 2018	Coinbene		OPEN
12th June 2019	DOBI		OPEN

COMMUNITY

A community is a network that shares common values, goals and dreams. The ARK Ecosystem has a community consisting of an innumerable number of people who have the project's wellbeing and future success at heart. The majority of these people prefer fictitious names with optional avatars.

There are platforms or websites on which the community discuss ideas, suggest improvements and post announcements related to the ARK Ecosystem. They are:

- https://bitcointalk.org/index.php?topic=1649695 Bitcointalk
- https://discord.ark.io Discord
- https://www.facebook.com/arkecosystem Facebook
- https://github.com/ArkEcosystem/ Github
- https://www.reddit.com/r/ArkEcosystem/ Reddit
- https://arkecosystem.slack.com Slack
- https://twitter.com/ArkEcosystem Twitter
- https://youtube.ark.io YouTube

Discussion takes place predominantly on the above Slack channel. It is the recommended place to engage with fellow members of the community, as well as receive support from knowledgeable core or community developers.

In essence, the community surrounding and participating in the development of the ARK Ecosystem is the backbone of the blockchain. Without a following, the prospects of future adoption and utilisation are starkly limited. The ARK Ecosystem belongs to all those who use it, not just to the developers who aid its progression.

ARK Ecosystem—Point. Click. Blockchain.

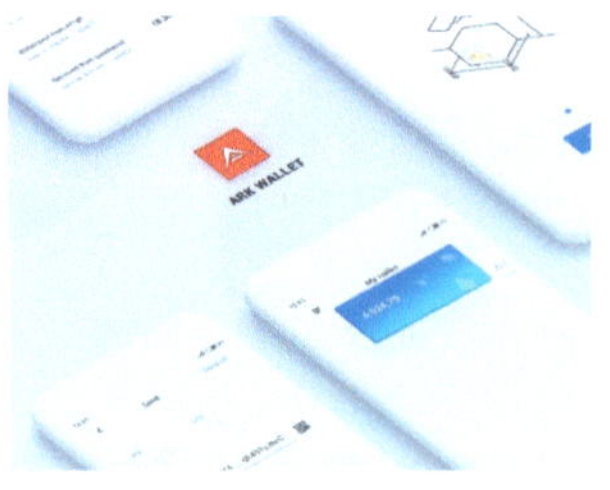

A CONCISE ARK ECOSYSTEM HISTORY

LIST OF CHAPTERS

I. **ARK ECOSYSTEM ANNOUNCED ON 15TH OCTOBER 2016**
II. **TOKEN EXCHANGE CAMPAIGN BEGAN ON 7TH NOVEMBER 2016**
III. **ARK SOURCE CODE MADE PUBLIC ON 12TH NOVEMBER 2016**
IV. **FIRST PUBLIC CORE TESTNET WENT LIVE ON 8TH DECEMBER 2016**
V. **TOKEN EXCHANGE CAMPAIGN ENDED ON 11TH DECEMBER 2016**

1

ARK EMBARKED ON THEIR VOYAGE

"ARK provides users with innovative use cases through the development and integration of technologies that power the blockchain universe."

In early September 2016, a passionate team consisting of over twenty individuals in fifteen different countries began to lay the foundations for a more efficient, robust and secure blockchain. This initial team, known as the ARK Co-founders, included François-Xavier Thoorens, Mike Doty, Travis Walker, Matthew D Cox, Lars Rensing, Rok Černec and Dr. Scott McPherson.

Using the codebase of a previously launched blockchain called Lisk (derived from Crypti and BitShares) as their starting point, the initial members of the ARK Crew began to collaborate and tirelessly test code to develop an ecosystem more heavily optimised for the needs of ARK users.

On the 15th October 2016 at 18:09:25 UTC, the official ARK Ecosystem Bitcointalk forum thread was created by Khanh Vuong. It was titled "ARK [PRE-ANN][ARK] Putting the Currency back into Crypto". It officially announced the project.

On the 25th October 2016, official ARK Ecosystem bounty campaigns were announced on related social media channels. All community members were free to support the initial promotion of the project by participating in the following:

- **Signature/Avatar Campaign (350,000 ARK):** Bitcointalk forum users had the opportunity to receive regular rewards for presenting official ARK signatures besides all their posted replies. It was a seven week campaign that ended on the 12th December 2016.
- **Sweepstakes (430,000 ARK):** By utilising the https://gleam.io service, the ARK Crew provided links to tasks such as liking Facebook and Twitter posts.
- **Translations (100,000 ARK):** Whoever successfully translated the official ARK Ecosystem announcement into one of twelve sought after languages, without using Google Translate, each received 8,000 ARK. All translations had to be complete at least two weeks before the end of the ARK TEC and had to be updated when necessary.
- **ARK Top Proposals Contest (300,000 ARK):** Technologically minded people were invited to propose unique and credible applications for potential development. The ARK Crew chose the best three ideas to fund.
- **ARK Supporting Websites (150,000 ARK):** After the mainnet ARK blockchain launched, any innovative websites promoting the benefits of ARK were each eligible to receive 5,000-20,000 ARK.
- **Github development or bug bounties (400,000 ARK):** Any developers willing to contribute to the development of the code were rewarded. Different reward tiers were listed depending on the size of the contribution.

In addition to the above bounties, others were available for the creation of blog articles (a total of 100,000 ARK rewarded and finished on 15th December 2016) and videos. A total of 2,500,000 ARK had been reserved for bounties. The ARK Crew promised to distribute all bounties immediately after the launch of the mainnet ARK blockchain. It was important for users to register an account at https://tec.ark.io before being able to receive their bounty rewards.

Besides the announcement of the ARK Ecosystem bounty campaigns, details of the upcoming ARK TEC (Token Exchange Campaign) were posted on the official Bitcointalk thread. It was also the day on which the first ARK Ecosystem whitepaper (version 1.0.1) titled "A Platform For Consumer Adoption" was published. It provided a more detailed understanding of the scope and vision of the project.

The ARK TEC was scheduled as a 35 day campaign to help raise funds, Bitcoin and Lisk, for ongoing code development and other operational activities. The community was assured that funds would be securely held by trusted third party escrows and released at a future time. As a reward for funding the ARK Ecosystem, people would receive ARK in accordance to the size of their contribution and how early they sent funds. The following table shows what bonuses were available:

Start Date	Finish Date	BTC Bonus (%)	LSK Bonus (%)
7th November 2016	8 November 2016	120	30
8th November 2016	13th November 2016	20	70
13th November 2016	20th November 2016	15	40
20th November 2016	27th November 2016	10	20
27th November 2016	4th December 2016	5	5
4th December 2016	11th December 2016	0	0

On the 7th November 2016, the official ARK Token Exchange Campaign began at https://tec.ark.io where people had to register in order to participate.

Initially, the plan was to raise a minimum of 2,000 BTC equivalent. The ARK Crew considered this sufficient to achieve recently set roadmap goals, to cover costs of development and to make ARK functionality a reality. It was stressed that the funds being raised were neither donations or investments, just receipts in exchange for native ARK coins (also referred to as usage tokens).

Within the first 24 hours, 569 participants had raised over 5,000,000 LSK and, as a whole, over US$1,000,000 in funds.

On the 12th November 2016 at 19:00 UTC, the ARK source code was uploaded to the official ARK Github repository website for the first time. It marked the start of the full open source philosophy of the project. Community developers became able to check, scrutinise and suggest alternatives to the code to make it more resilient, efficient and secure. The ARK Crew was quoted as saying:

> **"ARK is about inclusion, bringing people together, and creating something that can impact all of our lives in a meaningful way. To do that, we need you. We need everyone to get involved. We don't want ARK to be a project, we want it to be a movement. That is why we are officially announcing the release of the ARK source code to Github."**

Another major milestone occurred on the 25th November 2016. The initial pre-alpha ARK Desktop Wallet client (version 0.1.0) was released for Windows, Mac and Linux operating systems.

On the 8th December 2016, the first official ARK public testnet (ARK Core Alpha) went live. It was the culmination of many weeks of development. ARK Developers had worked long hours to stabilise the ARK Core on their internal test network. The ARK Crew invited community developers to download the software from the official ARK Ecosystem Github and help test the core network functions. It was time for the resilience and performance of the network to be tested in the real-world.

> **"The first Alpha release of the ARK core is a highly modified version of the Crypti/Lisk core client. Our development team has been hard at work removing unnecessary elements of the code and adding in several key improvements for stability that will facilitate the functionality required to create the first iteration of the SmartBridge."**

In addition to the testnet launch, relevant tutorial guides were published for those who required technical guidance for setting up nodes and registering delegates.

On the 11th December 2016, the ARK Token Exchange Campaign ended. The ARK Crew wholeheartedly appreciated all funds which had been raised (approximately 203 Bitcoin and 6,000,000 Lisk).

Taking into account that the minimum 2,000 BTC goal had not been reached, the ARK TEC website https://tec.ark.io was quickly modified to allow users to request a refund. The refund process was open for one week. The following final amounts of Bitcoin and Lisk were reimbursed to ARK TEC participants:

- On the 23rd December 2016, roughly 36 BTC had been refunded.
- On the 28th December 2016, roughly 1,300,000 LSK had been refunded.

After all reimbursements, roughly US$800,000 (167 BTC and 4,691,500 LSK) remained. Despite it not being what the team originally envisaged, there was still momentum to continue development.

On the 6th January 2017, designated third party escrow agents called Blazed and MalReynolds authorised the release of all 167 BTC (approx. US$150,000 at the time) from the TEC BTC wallet address to cover ARK development expenses (Lisk funds were released after the mainnet ARK blockchain launched).

After the holiday season, the capabilities and limitations of the ARK Core codebase were tested rigorously on the public testnet by both ARK developers and community developers. Many code bugs were discovered, then subsequently fixed.

During the first six weeks of 2017, the ARK Desktop Wallet testnet client was updated four times:

- On the 11th January 2017, version 0.2.0 was released. It was re-written from scratch due to substantial changes made to the ARK Core code.
- On the 20th January 2017, version 0.2.1 was released.
- On the 8th February 2017, version 0.3.0 was released. It improved the user friendliness of the client (easier to navigate).
- On the 13th February 2017, version 0.3.1 was released.

To the disappointment of some members of the community, the scheduled launch of the mainnet ARK blockchain did not occur on the 1st February 2017. It was delayed due to the time taken to fix several major ARK Core code bugs and to issue all TEC refunds. Despite this, the ARK Developers reported the public testnet as stable. It had become clear that there were lots of underlying issues that could only be fixed by re-writing major portions of the code. Ultimately, a solid launch of the mainnet ARK blockchain was being sought after.

Since the 24th December 2016, an ARK Art Design Contest had been running for talented designers to submit stunning images. A single winner was chosen each week for six weeks. In chronological order, the winners of the contest were sormin (see image below), densmirnov, jamiec79, mjbmonetarymetals, ICONEWS and CreativeEditors. Each winner received 5,000 ARK in prize money.

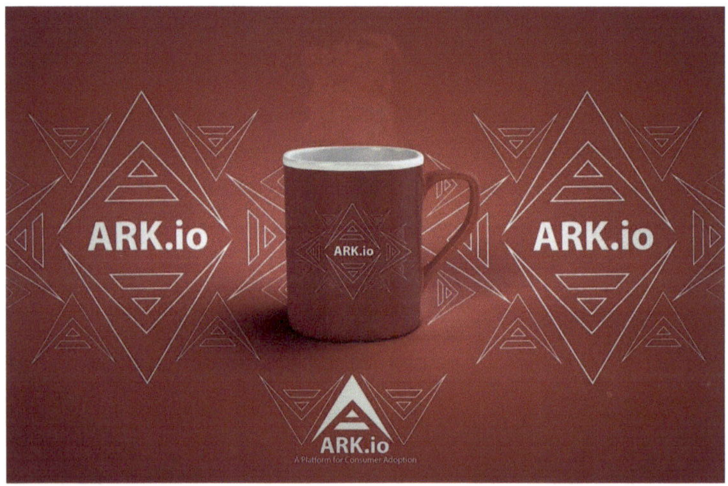

Towards the end of February 2017, the ARK Developers, lead by François-Xavier Thoorens, and community developers, were diligently working to optimise the core code. It was important to discover as many flaws as possible.

The launch of the mainnet ARK blockchain was not far away. Members of the community were encouraged to stay informed by visiting official ARK Ecosystem social media channels. In particular, people were welcome to sign up to the official Slack channel at https://arkecosystem.slack.com to talk to the ARK Crew.

Other events which occurred during this period included:

- On the 11th September 2016, both the official ARK Ecosystem Facebook and Slack social media channels were created.
- On the 12th September 2016, the official ARK Ecosystem Twitter account at https://twitter.com/ArkEcosystem went live.
- On the 11th October 2016, the official ARK Ecosystem Subreddit at https://www.reddit.com/r/ArkEcosystem was created.
- On the 1st December 2016, the beta version of the ARK Mobile Wallet was released only for testing purposes.
- On the 9th December 2016, an updated ARK Desktop Wallet (version 0.1.1) was released for testnet.
- On the 19th December 2016, the ARK Video Contest ended. A total of 40,000 ARK in prize money went to YouTuber Nippon Animation for a video titled "ARK - A PLATFORM FOR CONSUMER ADOPTION AD".
- On the 24th December 2016, the first official ARK Ecosystem online shop at https://shop.ark.io went live. It sells items such as ARK related t-shirts, mousepads, cups and customised Ledger hardware wallets.

I. **MAINNET ARK BLOCKCHAIN LAUNCHED ON 21ST MARCH 2017**

II. **DELEGATE FORGING REWARDS BEGAN ON 28TH MARCH 2017**

III. **SEVERAL DESKTOP WALLET CLIENT UPDATES WERE RELEASED**

IV. **ARK COMMUNITY FUND (ACF) COMMENCED ON 20TH MAY 2017**

V. **ARK PRICE SURPASSED US$1 FOR THE FIRST TIME ON 7TH JUNE 2017**

2

MAINNET BLOCKCHAIN LAUNCHED

"Overall we could not be more pleased. Very few glitches, no forks and the Bittrex trading volume skyrocketed shortly after launch, with rapid transfers from ARK wallets to Bittrex without any issues."

After several months of optimising the ARK Core code, the mainnet ARK blockchain launch date was announced on the 3rd March 2017. The date had been scheduled for the 21st March 2017. The ARK Crew praised all community developers who had helped to test the ARK Core code and ARK Desktop Wallet client on testnet.

"We would like to thank the community for being patient and sticking with us. This is just the beginning of what will be an amazing year for ARK. Mainnet launch is just the first milestone on an expansive development roadmap that we plan to continue to refine as we move forward."

The ARK Developers acknowledged that the development of the core code and desktop wallet client had taken more time than expected. They were pleased that stability had taken higher priority over speed of delivery. Stress testing was still occurring to discover any flaws before launch.

On the 21st March 2017, a few hours before launch, the first versions of the ARK Core and ARK Desktop Wallet (version 1.0.1) were released. Also, the ARK Commander utility tool was released to make it easier for users to install, configure and monitor ARK nodes.

Block #1 (Reward 125,000,000 ARK) March 21st 2017 at 19:00 UTC

As anticipated, the mainnet ARK blockchain successfully launched (see above) without any major issues. It also became possible for TEC participants to withdraw their ARK from https://tec.ark.io/dashboard to their own personal wallet addresses.

As promised, a cryptocurrency exchange initiated ARK trading on the same day as the mainnet ARK blockchain launched. Bittrex opened the ARK/BTC trading pair and became the first exchange to allow traders to buy or sell ARK. The first day of ARK/BTC trading volume on Bittrex was recorded at roughly 240 BTC (~US$264,000)

https://international.bittrex.com/Market/Index?MarketName=BTC-ARK

Bittrex is based in the USA and went live on the 14th February 2014. It is a trading platform committed to increase worldwide adoption of blockchain technology.

On the 22nd March 2017, ARK was added to the www.coinmarketcap.com ranking service. It is a website that primarily ranks over 2,000 cryptocurrencies (coins and tokens) in descending order of market capitalisation. It also presents useful charts, statistics and links to other cryptocurrency related material.

What follows is a table of historical data derived from www.coinmarketcap.com showing the first two days of recorded ARK prices:

	Low US$	Open US$	Close US$	High US$	Exch. Volume US$
22nd March 2017	0.030143	0.032677	0.034275	0.035979	133,793
23rd March 2017	0.032917	0.034463	0.058369	0.077314	825,848

On the 28th March 2017, delegate forging rewards began at block number 75,600 (see block below). The mainnet ARK blockchain shifted completely into the hands of the community. Delegate https://pool.arkno.de was the first forger of 2 ARK and was rewarded 2,000 ARK as a prize.

Block #75,600 (Reward 2 ARK) March 28th 2017 at 22:20:16 UTC

As appreciation for working tirelessly to test the core code before launch, the total of all transaction fees generated before block number 75,600 were evenly split between the 'magnificent seven'. They were dafty, michaelthecryptoguy, sidzero, ghostfaceuk, bcboilermaker, jamiec79 and toons. Matthew D Cox said:

> **"Today officially marked the beginning of Delegate Forging Rewards and our hard working delegates will now be rewarded for running the network nodes that power the ARK. The initiation of rewards was an exciting time for our delegates and we can't wait to see how the 51 forging positions shake out."**

On the 30th March 2017, the ARK Github Development Bounty Program was announced via the official blog. It began with immediate effect and opened to all community developers wishing to contribute to the ongoing testing and optimisation of the core code, desktop wallet client and other code ventures. A total of 200,000 ARK had been initially allocated towards rewarding the best contributors. The ARK Crew reiterated their commitment to the open source nature of the project and the importance of supporting the strong collaborative effort between the ARK Developers and the community.

Mainnet Blockchain Launched

On the 20th April 2017, the second major incentive program called '10 for 10,000' began to further enhance the ARK Ecosystem. Any ideas such as increasing the number of available programming languages in use for ARK or creating ARK payment plugins were suggested. Each accepted idea would receive 10,000 ARK on completion.

https://github.com/ArkEcosystem/ark-desktop/releases

Since the launch of the mainnet ARK blockchain, several ARK Desktop Wallet updates had been released. Lead developer François-Xavier Thoorens, alongside notable community developers including Lúcio Rubens, Kristjan Košič, jamiec79 and dafty, had worked hard to release the following in March, April and May 2017:

- On the 28th March 2017, version 1.0.2 improved the appearance of the client and fixed minor code bugs.
- On the 28th March 2017, version 1.1.0 added new features including the addition of a client restart notice when creating a second passphrase.
- On the 27th April 2017, version 1.2.0 improved transaction broadcasting across the network and fixed zero confirmation issues (resend ARK). It also added a feature to display the total BTC/fiat balance of all accounts.
- On the 10th May 2017, version 1.2.1 introduced features including the ability to see remaining balance, the option to send all ARK, a QR scanner for scanning a passphrase via a webcam and custom backgrounds.
- On the 12th May 2017, version 1.2.2 (hot-fix update to the previous version) resolved the issue of not being able to send decimal amounts of ARK.

On the 17th May 2017, the ARK Developers released an update to the ARK Core (version 1.0.1) for delegates or people running main ARK nodes. It was stressed that this did not effect regular ARK users using the ARK Desktop Wallet. It increased the preparation of the code for future deployable blockchains and multiple network support. The ARK Crew emphasised the importance of using ARK Desktop Wallet version 1.2.2 at the time.

An exciting ARK community initiative launched on the 20th May 2017. The ARK Community Fund, developed by the community for the community, was set up (created by jamiec79 and sidzero) to incentivise projects within the ARK Ecosystem. It received endorsement from the ARK Crew who donated an initial 25,000 ARK to support it. The initially elected ACF board members were dafty, jamiec79, toons, jarunik and michaelthecryptoguy. The ARK Community Fund is defined as follows:

"The ACF is an entirely community owned and operated vehicle for matching developers and entrepreneurs with potential seed funding through the use of the ARK Ecosystem. Potential projects will be able to submit applications to the team running the ACF to be considered for funding generated by an Active Delegate node as well donations from the ARK Community and Delegates."

https://arkcommunity.fund/

As a reward for extensively contributing to code development, Lúcio Rubens became the first major full-time addition to the ARK Core Development Team on the 1st June 2017. He fixed several code bugs and provided new features to the ARK Desktop Wallet client including 'Remaining Balance', 'Send All ARK' and the option to customise the background.

Lúcio Rubens is a stack developer from Brazil. After being hired to the ARK Crew, he was no longer eligible for Github Development Program bounties. It meant that more bounties became available for other community developers.

On the 7th June 2017, the ARK fiat price surpassed US$1 for the first time. It was also the day on which the ARK market capitalisation (the fiat value of all ARK in circulation) surpassed US$100,000,000. What follows is a table of historical data derived from www.coinmarketcap.com showing how quickly the ARK price ascended over three days:

	Low US$	Open US$	Close US$	High US$	Exch. Volume US$
5th June 2017	0.468821	0.503212	0.695637	0.741030	1,403,630
6th June 2017	0.534659	0.701361	0.802881	0.860576	2,902,360
7th June 2017	0.765574	0.804191	0.980932	1.24	5,115,610

To be specific, the following were simultaneously recorded on the 7th June 2017:

ARK Price: US$1.12 or 39,935 BTC Satoshi
ARK Market Capitalisation: US$107,259,611

At this time, it was possible for traders to buy and sell ARK on three cryptocurrency exchanges. They were Bittrex, Cryptopia and LiteBit.eu.

Other milestones set beforehand included:

- On the 13th April 2017, the ARK price surpassed US$0.10 for the first time.
- On the 13th April 2017, the Bitcoin Satoshi price per ARK went above 10,000 for the first time.
- On the 15th April 2017, the total daily ARK trading volume, over all recognised exchanges, was recorded over US$1,000,000 for the first time.

On the 22nd June 2017, block number 1,000,000 timestamped to the mainnet ARK blockchain. As soon as it occurred, a total of 1,848,802 ARK had been forged since forging began on 28th March 2017. This meant that 126,848,802 ARK had been generated so far.

Block #1,000,000 (Reward 2 ARK) June 22nd 2017 at 19:42:24 UTC

Other events which occurred during this period included:

- On the 22nd March 2017, the Cryptopia cryptocurrency exchange made it possible for its users to buy and sell ARK. It was an exchange based in New Zealand. In January 2019, it suffered a security breach and immediately ceased operations. It had been operational for just over four years (founded in December 2014).
- On the 22nd March 2017, ARK was added to the www.cryptocompare.com price metrics website.
- On the 7th April 2017, ARK was added to the www.bravenewcoin.com cryptocurrency data analytics website.
- On the 10th April 2017, ARK was added to the www.coingecko.com cryptocurrency analytics website.
- On the 24th April 2017, it became possible to buy, sell or store ARK on the www.litebit.eu exchange platform. It is based in The Netherlands.
- On the 9th June 2017, two ARK related trading pairs, ARK/BTC and ARK/ETH, went live on the https://coss.io trading exchange. On the 14th June 2018, the exchange opened the ARK/USD trading market.
- On the 21st June 2017, a real-time statistics website for the ARK network at https://arkstats.net went live. It was created by dafty.

I. DESKTOP WALLET V1.3.0 RELEASED ON 7TH AUGUST 2017

II. ARK INTEGRATED INTO LEDGER DEVICES ON 1ST SEPTEMBER 2017

III. DESKTOP WALLET V1.4.0 RELEASED ON 9TH OCTOBER 2017

IV. ARK BRANDING IMAGERY UPDATED IN OCTOBER 2017

V. ARK TRADING COMMENCED ON BINANCE ON 1ST NOVEMBER 2017

3

LEDGER HARDWARE WALLET INTEGRATION

"Ledger adds another layer of physical security and eliminates the need to input your entire passphrase when sending funds or voting from within the wallet."

Following weeks of discussion, the ARK Crew proudly announced a partnership with Ledger Hardware Wallets on the 5th July 2017. It resulted in ARK becoming the tenth cryptocurrency to be secured by the hardware. Especially, ARK was the first delegated proof of stake and first JavaScript blockchain to be integrated into Ledger. Ledger is described as follows:

"A fast paced, growing company developing security and infrastructure solutions for cryptocurrencies as well as blockchain applications for individuals and companies, by leveraging a distinctive, proprietary technology."

The ARK Crew also disclosed the 28th July 2017 as the date on which ARK would become fully integrated into Ledger devices such as the Ledger Nano S. The ARK Developers were busy updating the ARK Desktop Wallet for it to support and communicate with Ledger devices.

Unfortunately, the scheduled date for ARK integration into Ledger did not occur on the 28th July 2017. Ledger had been overwhelmed by issues related to the recent Bitcoin hard fork. François-Xavier Thoorens had been in direct talks with Ledger CEO Eric Larchevêque . They agreed upon the 1st September 2017 as the new date on which to integrate ARK.

On the 7th August 2017, ARK Desktop Wallet version 1.3.0 was released. It was described as a major update that introduced lots of new features, especially support for Ledger Hardware Wallets. The ARK Crew was quoted as saying:

> **"Once the Ledger team releases the upgrade to their software enabling ARK, you will simply need to connect your Ledger device to your computer and a new menu will be shown with your Ledger ARK address, from which you can send ARK."**

Other major features added to the wallet client, besides graphical user interface (GUI) improvements, included the following:

- Once a new version of the client is released, an icon will appear in the upper left corner displaying 'NEW VERSION AVAILABLE'.
- To choose local fiat currency displayed when sending ARK.
- To sign, verify and store messages to prove ownership of a wallet address.
- To select delegates from a drop-down menu instead of searching for them.
- To choose the colour theme of the wallet client.
- A sound effect corresponds to receiving ARK.
- An address book for recording contacts.
- To choose whether to show/hide the passphrase when typing it.

On the 1st September 2017, Oleg Shcherbyna became the second major hire to the ARK Crew. He had been hired to work full-time on the project. He is described as a UI/UX designer from the Ukraine.

Before he was hired, he had been creating unified designs for the ARK Ecosystem for the past several weeks. A decision was made to design more professional and consistent branding across all officially recognised social media channels and ARK Ecosystem websites (see image below and on page 51). It would inevitably attract the attention of people inside and outside the blockchain space.

On the 4th September 2017, ARK Desktop Wallet version 1.3.2 was released. It was a mandatory update for ARK users wishing to use a Ledger Nano S device for signing their ARK transactions. Three days before the release, Ledger Hardware Wallets officially integrated ARK at their end.

Other features integrated into ARK Desktop Wallet version 1.3.2 included:

- New fiat currency and language options.
- A new 'Select' option for fiat currencies.
- The ability to save/import a signed transaction file.
- Improved scrolling on the account dashboard.
- Removed 'type' column in the transaction list.

Besides François-Xavier Thoorens and Lúcio Rubens, community developers were congratulated for contributing to version 1.3.2 of the ARK Desktop Wallet. They were Stephen Bero, sleepdefic1t, Yago Antonio, Alex Beck, Naomi, Eugene Li, Brady, Matthew Cheung, zillionn and vekexasia.

Ledger Hardware Wallet Integration

On the 9th October 2017, ARK Desktop Wallet version 1.4.0 was released. It was the result of tireless coding from the ARK Development Team and community developers who had collaborated to fix numerous code bugs.

Major features integrated into this update included the following:

- Highly requested 'Dark Mode' preference.
- Automatically discovers Ledger ARK wallet addresses without loading the client each time.
- A splash screen is displayed when loading client content.
- When a Ledger Nano S device is connected, all ARK held in the device is automatically added to the total balance on the main dashboard.
- Underlying text is shown when a user hoovers over icons in account view.
- New ARK application, shortcut and desktop wallet title icons.
- The ability to save/export account history in .CSV file format.

Twelve community developers were praised for their contribution to version 1.4.0 of the ARK Desktop Wallet. They were Alex Barnsley, Juan A Martin, sleepdefic1t, Alex Beck, Chirag Khatri, Stephen Bero, Peter Ince, Noah Gregorio, Yago Antonio, Yohan Graterol, darfraider and Kristopher Rau.

For the past couple of months, Oleg Shcherbyna had been busy designing unified branding for all officially recognised online ARK Ecosystem material. The ARK Crew, and the community as a whole, applauded Oleg for his instrumental design skills and his success in aligning the project with what it envisages to achieve. Slack, Twitter, Facebook and Reddit accounts were all revamped.

On the 12th October 2017, the ARK Crew announced that all official ARK Ecosystem websites had been refreshed with the new branding imagery:

- The official website at https://ark.io had been completely revamped and re-coded. It became more simple, user friendly and aesthetically clean (see image below). Multi-lingual support was being worked on.
- The official block explorer at https://explorer.ark.io was re-coded from scratch to address high memory and CPU issues. Its functionality and feel were preserved with the addition of a 'Dark Mode' preference option.
- The official blog website at https://blog.ark.io began to present images designed in the same way.

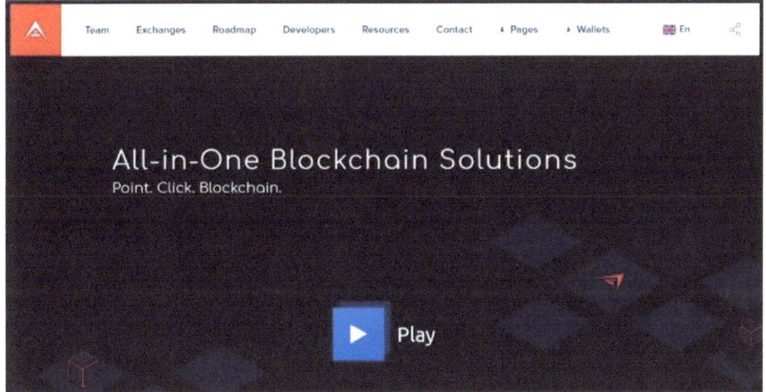

On the 24th October 2017, the Upbit cryptocurrency exchange commenced ARK trading by opening the ARK/BTC trading pair. A fiat trading pair, ARK/KRW, opened on the 18th November 2017.

https://upbit.com/exchange?code=CRIX.UPBIT.BTC-ARK
https://upbit.com/exchange?code=CRIX.UPBIT.KRW-ARK

Upbit is based in South Korea. It launched on the same day as ARK trading began with the help of a partnership with American based exchange called Bittrex.

On the 1st November 2017, ARK became available for trading on Binance, a top five international cryptocurrency exchange (at the time) in terms of trading volume. It was the first major Chinese exchange to initiate ARK trading. Binance opened two trading pairs, ARK/BTC and ARK/ETH, at the same time.

https://www.binance.com/en/trade/ARK_BTC
https://www.binance.com/en/trade/ARK_ETH

The ARK Crew described the addition to Binance as a major milestone. It helped to increase the exposure of the ARK Ecosystem. The following was posted:

> **"We would like to thank Binance for partnering with us, as this was a very long and much more difficult process than we both imagined. The integration of ARK was indeed a challenging process. As most exchanges are not used to custom blockchains like ARK, we had to design, develop, and integrate a new RPC (Remote Procedure Call) for Binance. From now on this RPC will streamline the addition process for other exchanges as well, making ARK easier to add and understand similar to bitcoin clones."**

Binance was founded in 2017 by Changpeng Zhao and Yi Hi in China. It is a platform on which over one hundred cryptocurrencies can be traded.

Over the preceding months, a significant number of community developers had enthusiastically participated in the Github Development Bounty Program. In particular, two talented full-stack developers were hired full-time to the ARK Crew in November 2017:

- On the 3rd November 2017, Juan A Martin joined the ARK Crew. He is from Spain.
- On the 14th November 2017, Alex Barnsley joined the ARK Crew. He is from the United Kingdom.

Other events which occurred during this period included:

- On the 6th August 2017, ARK was added to www.tradingview.com where it is possible to view real-time charts and statistics.
- On the 16th August 2017, ARK Desktop Wallet version 1.3.1 was released. It introduced features including the option for users to see their public keys.
- On the 29th August 2017, the number of people following the official ARK Twitter account surpassed 10,000 (see image below) for the first time.
- On the 5th September 2017, shipping of ARK branded Ledger Nano S hardware devices (limited to 1,000 units) began from https://shop.ark.io.
- On the 27th September 2017, the first Indian cryptocurrency exchange called BuyUcoin initiated ARK trading by creating the ARK/INR trading pair.
- On the 2nd October 2017, a UK based exchange called Cryptomate opened the first ARK/GBP trading pair.
- On the 10th October 2017, ARK Desktop Wallet version 1.4.1 was released. It resolved an issue related to the incorrectly displaying ARK total balance.
- On the 11th November 2017, Bit-Z became the second Chinese exchange to initiate ARK trading. It was founded in 2016 and based in Hong Kong, China.

I. **ARK INCORPORATED IN FRANCE ON 21ST NOVEMBER 2017**

II. **ALL TIME HIGH ARK FIAT PRICES WERE RECORDED**

III. **ARK MOBILE WALLET RELEASED ON 27TH DECEMBER 2017**

IV. **ARK DEPLOYER V1 (CLI) RELEASED ON 20TH JANUARY 2018**

V. **DESKTOP WALLET V1.5.0 RELEASED ON 25TH JANUARY 2018**

4

ARK MOBILE WALLET RELEASED

"We are happy to announce another huge achievement, with the release of the much awaited ARK Mobile Wallet. That's right, you can now vote for a delegate, send ARK, or just check your balance straight from the palm of your hand."

For nearly eight months, the mainnet ARK blockchain had been functioning without any major incidents. It had proven to be very fast and reliable. The ARK Crew was also pleased with how the community had grown and the organic growth in ARK transaction volume. Furthermore, the growing number of community developers participating in the Github Development Bounty Program was applauded.

"Throughout this time period, and with experience gained during the development of ARK, we have been able to identify several key elements in the core design that could be optimized. Now, we embark on a new voyage to completely overhaul the ARK core code as well as the protocol as a foundation of our ambitious roadmap."

On the 15th November 2017, the ARK Crew notified the community about their intention to re-write the ARK Core code from scratch (see quote above). The legacy Crypti/Lisk code had become too hard to work with. Work was underway to shift to a new codebase best suited to optimise the ARK Ecosystem in the future.

On the 18th November 2017, ARK Desktop Wallet version 1.4.2 was released. It fixed issues related to the back-end code to make the client more stable. It also integrated new features including:

- It became possible for wallet users to access the latest news articles from the official ARK blog from within the client (in the lower corner).
- The option to upload a personal custom background image to the client.
- When loading the client or switching network, a splash screen is visible.
- When the mouse hovers over an ARK address, the option to 'Copy Address' to clipboard becomes available.
- Once the number of confirmations is greater than fifty, the total number displayed is 'Well Confirmed' (hover over to see actual number).

Three days later, a 'hot-fix' update to the ARK Desktop Wallet (version 1.4.3) was released. It fixed problems with the unvoting process and made it easier to manage local fiat currency preferences.

As expected, the ARK Crew praised all community developers who had contributed to the ARK Desktop Wallet. They reiterated the benefits of different developer perspectives coding to make the client easier to use. Rok Černec, Alex Barnsley, Juan A Martin, Chirag Khatri, zillionn, Kristopher Rau, Sam Presnal, rbraunschweig, Noah Gregorio and Ardeshir81 were noted as contributors.

On the 21st November 2017, the ARK Ecosystem was incorporated in France as a co-operative society (SCIC) after intense investigative activity. A legal business entity was created to offer the structural framework for the ARK Ecosystem to successfully achieve its roadmap goals. The ARK Crew was quoted as saying:

> **"It is the first of its kind in the crypto world, and one of the first blockchain projects to incorporate in the European Union. We have been in close contact with the French financial governmental body and are keeping a very positive two way communication."**

The ARK Crew knew that it would help to speed up development and adoption, and inevitably increase the credibility of cryptocurrencies in France and beyond.

Without hesitation, a highly skilled core developer was announced as joining the ARK Crew on the 18th December 2017. Kristjan Košič was welcomed to the ARK Development Team as a blockchain enthusiast from Slovenia.

On the 20th December 2017, ARK became available for trading on OKEx, a top ten international cryptocurrency exchange (at the time) in terms of trading volume. OKEx opened three ARK related trading pairs (see below) on the same day.

https://www.okex.com/market?product=ark_btc
https://www.okex.com/market?product=ark_eth
https://www.okex.com/market?product=ark_usdt

OKEx was founded in 2014 and is based in Malta. It is a platform on which over one hundred cryptocurrencies can be traded.

Since ARK trading began on the open trading markets, the ARK price had been increasing in a similar manner to many other cryptocurrencies. Bitcoin, Ethereum, Ripple, Litecoin, to name a few, were recording all time highs.

What follows is a table of historical data derived from www.coinmarketcap.com showing the astronomical rise in ARK price since April 2017. On the 21st December 2017, the all time 2017 high ARK price was recorded at US$9.11 (52,996 Bitcoin Satoshi) over all recognised exchanges. On this day, Bitcoin and Ethereum attained highs (not all time highs) at US$17,567.70 and US$880.54 respectively.

	Low US$	Open US$	Close US$	High US$	Exch. Volume US$
21st April 2017	0.229602	0.243008	0.241915	0.253126	192,799
21st June 2017	0.602867	0.687254	0.655538	0.724148	554,921
21st August 2017	1.63	1.65	1.80	1.95	4,416,240
21st October 2017	2.41	2.78	2.57	2.79	2,184,140
21st December 2017	7.33	7.44	7.89	9.11	20,930,800

ARK Mobile Wallet Released

On the 27th December 2017, the first ever ARK Mobile Wallet application (version 1.0.1) was released. It was described as a huge achievement. It became possible for users of the ARK Ecosystem to use features such as delegate voting and sending ARK whilst on the go. The ARK Developers highlighted the beta nature of the software.

Lúcio Rubens was praised for taking the lead in its development. Alex Barnsley was congratulated for assisting Lúcio and Oleg Shcherbyna designed its format.

At this time, only a version for Android was available. A version for iOS devices was still pending review from Apple.

https://github.com/ArkEcosystem/mobile-wallet/releases

On the 9th January 2018, ARK Desktop Wallet version 1.5.0 was released. It improved the user interface for voting and unvoting delegates. Other new features integrated into this version were:

- The client automatically checks whether the inputted ARK wallet address is valid. It will not prevent ARK from being sent to an invalid address, but will ask the user if s/he would rather send the ARK to another address.
- The ability to export all transactions to a .CSV file (no longer limited to just 50 transactions).
- The ability to quickly switch from selected fiat currency to Bitcoin on the main dashboard.

As always, community developers were applauded for contributing to the code of the ARK Desktop Wallet above. They included Sam Presnal, nascius, Chirag Khatri, zillionn, Perry Hoffman, Steven Huijgens and Jonas Zuberbuehler.

On the 20th January 2018, the first official ARK Deployer was made available. The first steps had been taken towards making it easier to prepare, customise and deploy an ARK based blockchain. At this time, the application was only command line (CLI) best suited for technically minded users of the ARK Ecosystem. The ARK Deployer was defined, at the time of its release, as follows:

> **"It is a lightweight deployment script for creating your own ARK based blockchains. By utilizing the ARK Deployer, developers can create their own blockchain in a matter of minutes. ARK Deployer is just the first step in building a more robust ecosystem that will be user friendly, customizable, and will feature the same calibre of user experience you have all come to expect from an ARK project."**

The ARK Deployer later became a tool at hackathons for programmers to learn how the ARK Ecosystem works. Alex Barnsley had led the development of the ARK Deployer with help from Brian Faust.

On the 14th February 2018, Jeremy Epstein joined the ARK Crew as a marketing advisor to help CMO Travis Walker. His passion for the ability and potential of blockchain technology was acknowledged and applauded. He later amicably departed the ARK Crew on the 14th June 2018.

Other events which occurred during this period included:

- On the 25th December 2017, the ARK Ecosystem formed a partnership with a decentralised trading platform called Blockport.
- On the 9th January 2018, the all time 2018 high ARK price was recorded at US$10.92 (74,152 Bitcoin Satoshi).
- On the 16th-18th January 2018, members of the ARK Crew attended the North American Bitcoin Conference in Miami, Florida, USA. Dr. Scott McPherson gave a fifteen minute presentation about the ARK Ecosystem.
- On the 25th January 2018, ARK Desktop Wallet version 1.5.1 was released. It integrated a feature to make it easier for merchants or websites to accept ARK as a means of payment (web component to generate QR codes).
- On the 30th January 2018, the exchange Abucoins initiated ARK trading.

I. **FIRST OFFICIAL ARK CON TOOK PLACE IN ARCHAMPS, FRANCE**

II. **ARK BLOCKCHAIN FIRST YEAR ANNIVERSARY ON 21ST MARCH 2018**

III. **ARK CREW HAD ATTENDED AND SPONSORED HACKATHONS**

IV. **CONSENSUS 2018 IN NEW YORK CITY BEGAN ON 14TH MAY 2018**

V. **CONSENSUS 2018 IN NEW YORK CITY ENDED ON 16TH MAY 2018**

5

CONSENSUS 2018 IN NEW YORK CITY

"Consensus 2018 was a massive hit and by far one of the biggest events in the industry. This years event was full of excitement and innovative solutions that show not only is blockchain here to stay, but it's about to take the world by storm."

Besides transitioning to a more advanced codebase, the ARK Crew announced on the 22nd February 2018 that they had begun to develop version 2.0.0 of the ARK Desktop Wallet. The ARK Developers reported that the Angular 1 (JavaScript) framework used to develop 1.x versions had become too restrictive. An alternative JavaScript Framework called Vue.js had been chosen to develop version 2.0.0 and deliver the following:

- It will increase the number of contributors to the code (more simple).
- It will use less resources (higher performance)
- It will be easier to review code changes (easier to maintain and fix)

At the time, maintenance of the current ARK Desktop Wallet (version 1.5.1) would continue, but only to fix critical bugs or implement useful features.

Consensus 2018 in New York City

During the first three months of 2018, the ARK Crew attended several conferences with the aim to showcase the ARK Ecosystem. Each conference event was an opportunity to present the vision of the project, and answer questions from interested third parties, ARK supporters and general attendees. The first three conferences sponsored and attended by the ARK Crew in 2018 were:

- On the 16th-18th January 2018, they attended The North American Bitcoin Conference in Miami, Florida, USA. (ARK Ecosystem was a Gold Sponsor).
- On the 22nd-24th February 2018, they attended Blockchain & Crypto Con 2018 in Dallas, Texas, USA (ARK Ecosystem was a Diamond Sponsor).
- On the 15th-16th March 2018, they attended Token Fest at The Palace of Fine Arts Theatre in San Francisco, California, USA.

In addition to attending the three conferences above, the ARK Crew came together to celebrate the first year anniversary of the mainnet ARK blockchain in Archamps, France on the 21st-24th March 2018. It was the first ever official ARK Ecosystem conference or meetup. As well as being a joyous occasion, its purpose was:

> **"Our goal for this event is to discuss the way forward and our roadmap for 2018, the SCIC business structure, as well as the future of blockchain and how ARK can be ambassadors to promote common sense, pro-blockchain regulation to make France a desired destination for blockchain companies."**

On the 21st March 2018, François-Xavier Thoorens spoke on stage about the history, merits and future goals of the ARK Ecosystem in front of an audience intrigued in the blockchain technology space.

On the 22nd March 2018, the ARK Crew welcomed community members, delegates and developers (maximum of one hundred people) to meet the team. It was a great opportunity to ask questions and discuss the ARK Ecosystem face-to-face.

As shown below, block number 3,892,526 marked the time at which the mainnet ARK blockchain had been operational for one year.

Block #3,892,526 (Reward 2 ARK) March 21st 2018 at 19:00 UTC

On the 4th April 2018, Simon Downey (also known as sleepdefic1t) joined the ARK Crew as a full-time developer from the community. He was also the first official hire to the IoT ARK Development Team.

On the 1st May 2018, another talented person was announced as joining the ARK Crew. Adrian Kerchev was hired as a networking architect from Bulgaria.

For the past year, the ARK Crew had been attending and sponsoring hackathons in the United States and Europe. Hackathons are events at which programmers, especially young people, participate in workshops with the goal of coding interesting applications. The ARK Crew attended eight major hackathons from June 2017 to May 2018. They included the following:

22nd-23rd June 2017
HACKUC in Scotch Plains, New Jersey, USA

20th-22nd October 2017
JSHacks 'Bucharest Blockchain Edition' JavaScript Hackathon in Romania

10th-12th November 2017
HackPrinceton—A Major League Hacking's Season at Princeton University

20th-21st January 2018
Hack Cambridge Hackathon at Cambridge University in the UK

30th March—1st April 2018
HackPrinceton 2018 Spring

6th-8th April 2018
Bitcamp Hackathon in the Xfinity Center at the University of Maryland, USA

12th-14th April 2018
Open Geneva Hackathon in Switzerland

5th-6th May 2018
BlockHack at Delaware University, USA

Hackathon events are opportunities for the ARK Crew to educate, engage with and encourage bright young programmers. One core mission of the ARK Ecosystem is to spread awareness of blockchain technology, especially the aspects of the mainnet ARK blockchain and using the ARK Deployer to create custom bridgechains.

Consensus 2018 in New York City

On the 16th-18th May 2018, the ARK Ecosystem attended and sponsored a major conference in the blockchain technology space called Consensus 2018. It took place at the New York Hilton Midtown in Manhattan, New York City.

It was reported that over 8,500 people attended the conference. Most attendees were enthusiastic to learn more about innovative blockchain projects, be part of the excitement and forge new relationships. The ARK Crew described their time there as amazing as they met, and talked with, thousands of people and multiple ARK Delegates. Other key highlights during the three day conference were:

- Delegate biz_classic supplied a physical ARK faucet sink from which attendees were able to receive small amounts of free ARK directly to their mobiles or paper wallets via QR codes.
- François-Xavier Thoorens, Dr. Scott McPherson and Jeremy Epstein gave presentations in a private room.
- One thousand bags of ARK swag were handed out. Each bag contained items such as ARK branded stickers, water bottles, t-shirts and much more.

Overall, the conference was a massive success. The ARK Ecosystem was heavily promoted by many banners, posters and wall wraps presenting the 'All-in-One' slogan. They also received lots of praise and positive feedback.

After the conference in New York City, the focus shifted to the upcoming ARK Core V2 code release. There were many other exciting things to look forward to for the remainder of the year.

Other events which occurred during this period included:

- On the 5th March 2018, ARK Co-founder Stefan Neagu attended the ToFinance Student Conference in Romania.
- On the 12th March 2018, ARK Mobile Wallet version 1.1.0 was released. It introduced many new features to make the application more user friendly.
- On the 13th March 2018, three trading pairs, ARK/BTC, ARK/ETH and ARK/USD, went live on the Livecoin cryptocurrency exchange.
- On the 26th March 2018, ARK trading began on the GODEX exchange.
- On the 15th May 2018, SimpleSwap integrated ARK into their platform to allow users to buy/sell ARK without registering an account.
- On the 21st May 2018, ARK trading began on the Exrates.me exchange.
- On the 25th May 2018, it became possible to instantly and seamlessly exchange ARK on Changelly. Changelly is a service that allows people to buy over 150 different cryptocurrencies by acting as an intermediary between exchanges and users. It has been operational since 2015.

I. **FIRST ARK CORE V2 DEVNET VERSION RELEASED ON 14TH JUNE 2018**

II. **SEVEN TEAM PLAYERS HIRED TO THE ARK CREW**

III. **SEVERAL PARTNERSHIPS FORMED**

IV. **NEW V2 ONLY DEVNET LAUNCHED ON 15TH AUGUST 2018**

V. **MOBILE WALLET V1.2 RELEASED ON 13TH SEPTEMBER 2018**

6

ARK CREW EXPANSION

"ARK would be nothing without our community and we are proud to have you all on this journey with us. We are poised to begin a new chapter in ARK history and we wouldn't want to do it without you!"

Since November 2017, the ARK Developers had been developing and testing the ARK Core V2 codebase on their private internal test network. On the 31st May 2018, the official release date of public testing on the DevNet test network was announced (14th June 2018).

The ARK Developers highlighted the fact that the first iteration of ARK Core V2 was being developed to be 100% backward compatible with version one. It would therefore be possible to run old nodes on the public DevNet, but the ARK Crew recommended testers to switch to running new nodes as soon as possible.

On the 14th June 2018, as promised, the first publicly available ARK Core V2 DevNet launched without major problems. All relevant downloads were made available via the official ARK Ecosystem Github repository website. The backward compatibility of the code with version one was honoured. Work was underway to thoroughly test the code in order to discover, report and fix bugs. As always, community developers were encouraged to contribute to the open source nature of the project. On the 14th June 2018, the ARK Crew posted the following:

> **"The entire ARK team would like to thank our core developers who spent numerous hours brainstorming, developing, implementing and testing the new Core! We are truly grateful and hope you guys keep on rocking like you do."**

Also on the 14th June 2018, ARK Core Commander V2 was released. It had also been re-written from scratch. Tutorial guides were published to show how to utilise it. It was defined as follows:

> **"ARK Core 2.0 Commander is a tool set that helps ARK node operators quickly install the ARK Core along with all necessary dependencies required. Node configuration, operation and maintaining functions are also provided. This eliminates the inconvenience of manual command line entry."**

To help the community understand the ARK Ecosystem, an enthusiastic member of the community called Justin Renken (before he joined the ARK Crew) uploaded a video presentation titled "ARK Blockchain Ecosystem Overview" to YouTube. He covered an array of ARK Ecosysyem concepts (see the screenshot below) for an approximate eight minute time period.

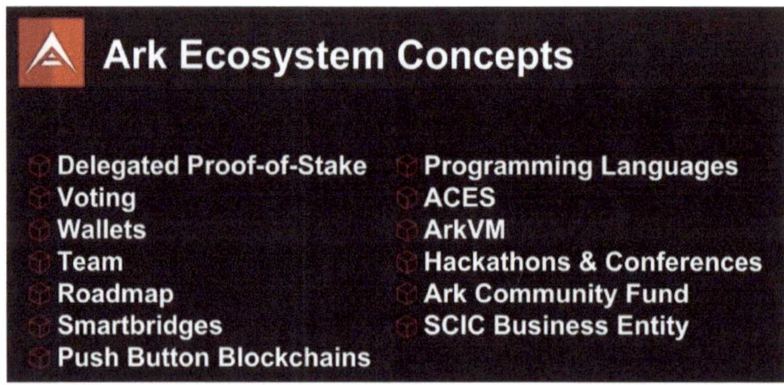

Also known by his alias Doubled1c3, Justin Renken thanked all community members who had viewed the presentation. It was sponsored by the ARK Community Fund (ACF) and ARK Stickers.

On the 27th June 2018, ARK Desktop Wallet version 1.6.0 was released. It had been almost five months since the previous update. It was also described as the last 1.x update due to the fact that the ARK Developers were busy developing ARK Desktop Wallet version 2 from scratch.

Several new features were integrated into the above update thanks to help from community developers including nascius, zillionn, Gabriel Bull, Dunnen, Supaiku and trigger67:

- Changelly was directly integrated to make it easier for users to purchase ARK with fiat currency from within the client.
- It became possible for users to load and send multiple transactions by using a .CSV file.
- To generate and import a passphrase in all possible BIP39 languages.

On the 24th July 2018, after much thought and deliberation, the ARK Crew notified the community about the following:

> **"For the past few weeks we have been testing the new ARK Core v2 software along with the intended v1 backwards compatibility on our internal TestNet and public DevNet. And ... the two versions do not play well together. The spaghetti left over from the legacy code of Lisk, and prior to that Crypti, is causing too much heartache and even more headaches."**

It was therefore necessary to release a new V2 only public DevNet and then focus on migrating to ARK Core V2 on the mainnet ARK blockchain as soon as possible.

On the 30th July 2018, Matthew D Cox published an official ARK blog article in which he advertised vacant ARK Crew positions, especially for a Communications Engagement Manager. He encouraged people already active within the community to submit applications detailing their skills and experience. It was time to heavily increase the size of the ARK Crew.

It had reached the point at which the ARK Co-founders wanted to spend more time showcasing the capabilities of the ARK Ecosystem. There was also eagerness to focus on forming new partnerships and building the ARK vision according to set roadmap goals. With the upcoming release of ARK Core V2, it was vital to hire more people to help the ARK Ecosystem grow during a more demanding time.

On the 31st July 2018, the ARK price went below US$1 for the first time since the 14th August 2017. It had decreased by over 90% from its all time high recorded at the beginning of the year. Despite this, the ARK Crew and the community did not become demoralised or deterred from pursuing their long term goals.

What follows is a table of historical data derived from www.coinmarketcap.com showing how much the ARK price decreased during the last two days of July 2018:

	Low US$	Open US$	Close US$	High US$	Exch. Volume US$
30th July 2018	1.14	1.25	1.17	1.25	610,393
31st July 2018	0.991732	1.18	1.01	1.18	1,456,300

On the 15th August 2018, the new (version two only) public DevNet went live:

> **"With the recent announcement of the ARK Core V2 hard fork, we have decided to prepare a v2 only DevNet that will help us squash any final bugs in the codebase. We need help from you, the community, to join us in testing all transaction types, edge cases, stress test and to help us improve things we might have missed by reporting any unusual behaviour."**

Since the announcement to increase the size of the ARK Crew, five people joined the core team in July and August 2018. They were:

- On the 31st July 2018, Gerard Blezer became a new member of the finance team (Finance & Compliance Manager) to assist CFO Lars Rensing.
- On the 1st August 2018, Carlye Wicklund became a Community Support Specialist. She had helped the ARK Ecosystem at conferences.
- On the 13th August 2018, Justin Renken filled the Communications Specialist role. He had proven to be a highly active community member with immense enthusiasm and confidence. He had been running ARK Stickers.
- On the 14th August 2018, Mario Vega (Technical Writer & Developer) began to write simple and in-depth tutorials based on ARK Ecosystem technicalities.
- On the 20th August 2018, Erwann Gentric joined the ARK Core Development Team. He had been very active in the Github Development Bounty Program.

Besides expanding the ARK Crew, several partnerships were formed during summer 2018. They were announced on the following dates:

- On the 25th July 2018, the ARK Ecosystem partnered with Hiway.io. It is a blockchain based hiring platform used to help find qualified people in the blockchain technology space.
- On the 23rd August 2018, the ARK Ecosystem partnered with Ø Crypto Union. It makes it possible to borrow fiat money by using ARK as collateral.
- On the 27th August 2018, the ARK Ecosystem partnered with MARAChain. It is a secure platform for transferring (GDPR-compliant) digital documents.
- On the 6th September 2018, the ARK Ecosystem partnered with Major League Hacking. It is a company that operates a league of student hackathons. It was founded in 2013 by Mike Swift and Jonathan Gottfried.

Partnerships continue to be a key component of the ARK vision. The ARK Crew proudly co-operate with others in order to increase blockchain adoption.

On the 13th September 2018, ARK Mobile Wallet version 1.2 was released. It was the first update since the 12th March 2018. It integrated features including:

- The ability to add ARK based blockchains or bridgechains to the application.
- Highly requested 'Dark Mode' preference.
- Compatibility with the V2 only public DevNet.
- The ability to validate passphrases (BIP39) when importing accounts.
- To generate and import passphrases in all possible BIP39 languages.
- It became possible for users to hide/show the passphrase while inputting.
- An option to enter how much ARK the user would like to receive.
- When a wallet address is removed, the user has to enter their PIN.

In addition to the above features, six new language options were added. They were French, Korean, Bulgarian, Czech, Italian and Portuguese.

Building on the recent hires to the ARK Crew during the summer, two talented core developers joined the team in September 2018 on a full-time basis:

- On the 3rd September 2018, Joshua Noack joined the team. Before he was hired, he had worked as a full-time developer on C++/Qt embedded systems.
- On the 24th September 2018, Vasil Dimov became the fourth core developer to be hired during the preceding two months. He is from Bulgaria.

The migration to ARK Core V2 on the mainnet ARK blockchain was still scheduled to take place before the end of the year. It was necessary to carry out further testing. For instance, the ARK Developers had plans to subject the ARK Core V2 codebase to high transaction volumes and test the Dynamic Fees feature.

Other events which occurred during this period included:

- On the 31st May 2018, Apple approved the iOS ARK Mobile Wallet. It became available for download from the App Store on the same day.
- On the 13th June 2018, the ARK Docs website at https://docs.ark.io went live. It is a hub consisting of tutorial guides and other information.
- On the 12th-13th July 2018, the ARK Crew attended (and sponsored) Korea Blockchain Summit 2018. Dr Scott McPherson gave a presentation.
- On the 20th July 2018, ARK Desktop Wallet version 1.6.1 was released.
- On the 25th July 2018, the ARK/BTC trading pair opened on Coinbene.
- On the 14th August 2018, the ARK Crypto Podcast debuted and became accessible at https://thearkcryptopodcast.com. It is hosted by Justin Renken and produced by Matthew D Cox. It is a weekly podcast (see image below) for the community to listen to material related to the ARK Ecosystem. It is also an educational resource, but not investment advice.
- On the 19th-20th September 2018, five members of the ARK Crew, Matthew D Cox, Travis Walker, Lars Rensing, Rok Černec and Dr. Scott McPherson attended Consensus 2018 in Singapore. They talked face-to-face with the Changelly team and it was the first time Matthew D Cox met the other ARK Crew members in person.

I. **ARK V2 TESTATHON TOOK PLACE IN EARLY NOVEMBER 2018**

II. **MIGRATION TO ARK CORE V2 BEGAN ON 28TH NOVEMBER 2018**

III. **DESKTOP WALLET V2.0.0 RELEASED ON 3RD DECEMBER 2018**

IV. **ARK CORE V2 MIGRATION ENDED ON 4TH DECEMBER 2018**

V. **DESKTOP WALLET V2.1.0 RELEASED ON 14TH DECEMBER 2018**

7

ARK CORE V2 WENT LIVE ON MAINNET

"Migration to the new ARK Core v2 has been successfully completed on Mainnet. With this milestone, we begin a new era of ARK development and have a foundation for a more stable and efficient network."

ARK Core V2 code development and testing had progressed as envisaged over the past several months. On the 28th September 2018, the ARK Developers highlighted four areas of the code to test during October 2018. They invited delegates and community developers to help test the following:

- **Multi-signatures**—configurating wallets and sending transactions via CLI
- **Dynamic Fees**—testing different transaction fee scenarios via CLI
- **Stress Testing**—testing resilience by mass spamming the network with transactions, massive voting and unvoting of delegates etc.
- **Other tests**—forking, double forging, testing snapshots

It was important to test the full functionality and limitations of the new core code before migrating to it on the mainnet ARK blockchain.

Besides testing ARK Core V2 in October 2018, the ARK Crew was busy promoting the project by giving presentations or participating in interviews:

- On the 2nd October 2018, François-Xavier Thoorens gave a presentation at DevChain in Geneva, Switzerland.
- On the 2nd October 2018, Travis Walker was interviewed by David Gil on The Edge Podcast.
- On the 16th October 2018, Justin Renken spoke about the ARK Ecosystem at the Blockchain NW Summit in Seattle, Washington, USA.
- On the 18th October 2018, Lars Rensing was interviewed by Dutch based Satoshi Radio.
- Both Justin Renken and Travis Walker attended the World Crypto Conference at the Aria Casino Resort in Las Vegas, Nevada, USA from 31st October to the 2nd November 2018.

On the 1st November 2018 at 07:00 UTC, the ARK V2 Testathon began as the final testing phase before mainnet migration. Community developers were incentivised to submit code issues or provide solutions for a chance to receive ARK (denominated in US Dollars). To make it more appealing, all those who submitted at least one accepted fix or solution were entered into a future draw with the chance to win a limited edition ARK engraved Ledger Nano S device.

On the 8th November 2018 at 07:00 UTC, the ARK V2 Testathon ended. The ARK Crew was quoted as saying:

> **"We would like to thank each and every person who helped test the new Core — be it reporting issues or, providing solutions, helping with running devnet nodes or just providing moral support in the channel. Thank you all."**

On the 15th November 2018 at 16:00 UTC, both dated and JeremiGendron were randomly chosen via www.randomresult.com as winners of the ARK V2 Testathon Ledger Nano S Competition. Four other entrants into the draw were paroxysm, zillionn, thomas-neuman and wownmedia.

On the 28th November 2018, the highly anticipated migration of the mainnet ARK blockchain to version two began. ARK Core V2 was released on the same day at 16:00 UTC for delegates to download, synchronise (from block number 0) and validate over the course of five days. It was considered ample time for them to prepare their servers before the switch.

On the 3rd December 2018 at 16:00 UTC, the switch to ARK Core V2 occurred. All delegates came to agreement, switched off their old node servers and began forging blocks compatible with the new core codebase. At this time, all version one servers had gone offline.

After the ARK Developers had had time to monitor the performance of the network, a few hours later, on the 3rd December 2018, ARK Desktop Wallet version 2.0.0 was released for download via the Github repository website and other official websites.

What follows are some new features integrated into the update:

- It become possible for wallet users to choose the transaction fee when sending ARK via the Dynamic Fees feature. It was the case that transactions sent using version one fees would still confirm almost immediately.
- An option to encrypt the passphrase with a custom password. Users sign and verify transactions with the custom password which decrypts the passphrase stored on the user's personal computer.
- The ability to read official ARK blog articles without leaving the wallet client.
- The ability to create different profiles.
- The integration of an ARK market chart.

As mentioned or discussed at length, the desktop wallet released above had also been re-written from scratch. Vue.js and TailwindCSS had been used resulting in a better user experience.

Block #6,600,000 (Reward 2 ARK) December 4th 2018 at 15:09:22 UTC

As planned, block number 6,600,000 (see above) marked the time at which the mainnet ARK blockchain began to automatically accept a maximum of 150 transactions per block or just over 19 transactions per second. The first block containing over 50 transactions activated the protocol change after which any remaining version one nodes forked. Migration to ARK Core V2 was complete.

On the 11th December 2018, Sam Harper-Pittam joined the ARK Crew as a Community Engagement Manager from the United Kingdom. He began to be responsible for building relationships within the community and moderating discussions on ARK related social media channels such as Slack, Reddit and Discord.

After nearly two weeks of feedback from the community, ARK Desktop Wallet version 2.1.0 was released on the 14th December 2018. It implemented new features including:

- The ability to customise the names of ARK wallet addresses.
- The total balance of all ARK wallet addresses, including connected Ledger hardware wallets, displayed at the top of the wallet overview page.
- The re-integration of the Changelly feature for users to purchase ARK from within the wallet client.
- All transactions listed show the full date and time sent.
- A banner displays at the bottom of the overview page showing which delegates, and the delegate rank, the user is currently voting for.
- Searching for recipient changed to case insensitive (better user experience)
- The ability to disable the market chart on the dashboard.

Other enhancements were made to the user interface to make it easier to navigate and more aesthetically clean. Github contributors who had helped to develop the update were Edgar Zoetzendorff (@dated), Michel Kraaijeveld (@ItsANameToo), zillionn, highjhacker, kalgoop and JeremiGendron.

Other events which occurred during December 2018 included:

- On the 5th December 2018, ARK Mobile Wallet version 1.3.1 was released for Android devices (first ARK Core V2 compatible version).
- On the 8th December 2018, ARK Mobile Wallet version 1.3.1 was released for iOS devices (first ARK Core V2 compatible version).
- On the 10th December 2018, the ARK Ecosystem formed a collaborative partnership with Bugcrowd. Bugcrowd is a crowd sourced security platform that helps companies discover critical code issues.
- On the 21st December 2018, ARK Desktop Wallet version 2.1.1 was released for users wishing to utilise the ARK Pay feature.
- On the 21st December 2018, ARK Pay was introduced as a simple JavaScript plug-in to provide merchants with a tool to easily accept ARK as a form of online payment.

There was consensus that 2018 had been a very productive and exciting year. It was time to take a well-deserved break. Core members of the ARK Crew wished the community a "Merry Arkmas" in an official ARK Ecosystem YouTube video.

At the end of 2018, ARK Core V2 had been functioning well for four weeks. It was full steam ahead to improve the code and add new features in 2019.

I. **MOBILE WALLET V1.4.0 RELEASED ON 8TH FEBRUARY 2019**

II. **JUSTIN RENKEN CONTINUED TO PROMOTE THE ARK ECOSYSTEM**

III. **FIVE ARK DESKTOP WALLET UPDATES WERE RELEASED**

IV. **ARK DEPLOYER V2 (CLI) WENT LIVE ON 18TH MARCH 2019**

V. **ARK WHITEPAPER V2 PUBLISHED ON 5TH APRIL 2019**

8

WHITEPAPER V2 PUBLISHED

"Today, ARK speaks with a unified voice with the release of an all-new ARK Ecosystem whitepaper. The whitepaper represents months of team-wide collaboration and years of achievement and progress."

Without becoming complacent after the successful migration to ARK Core V2 on the mainnet ARK blockchain, the ARK Developers assured the community that code development would speed up. Improvements to the core codebase had already been set in motion. In particular, the final stages of migrating the codebase from JavaScript to TypeScript had begun. TypeScript is defined as:

"TypeScript is an open-source programming language developed and maintained by Microsoft. It is a strict syntactical superset of JavaScript, and adds optional static typing to the language. TypeScript is designed for development of large applications and transcompiles to JavaScript."

As always, participation and feedback from the community was encouraged. The ARK Crew emphasised, as had been stated numerous times before, that the ARK Ecosystem would continue to pride itself on the open source nature of its codebase.

On the 4th January 2019, the ARK Github Development Bounty Program was revised to prioritise quality over quantity. Community developers still had the ability to claim rewards for discovering code flaws or providing fixes. It was highlighted that most developers who were part of the ARK Crew had been hired from the program.

On the 17th January 2019, ARK Desktop Wallet version 2.2.0 was released. It fixed issues with the code and integrated features including:

- The ability to switch between grid view and list view on the wallet addresses and contacts pages.
- A completely revamped profile creation page.
- When viewing a wallet address, the user can add it to their contacts list by clicking the 'Add to Contacts' button.
- When sending all funds from a specific wallet address, the user is prompted with a pop-up window for verification.
- Shows a message if the wallet is a known verified wallet address.
- An option to broadcast to multiple peers. If selected, a transaction will be broadcast to the 10 best peers, 5 random peers and 5 random seed peers.
- Time presented in the wallet now matches that of the ARK Explorer.
- An option to keep the current avatar or the first letter of the profile name as your avatar.

Since the previous ARK Desktop Wallet update, ten developers had contributed by adding 4,997 and deleting 1,234 lines of code. Community developers who contributed to it included Edgar Goetzendorff (@dated), zillionn, kalgoop, Michel Kraaijeveld (@ItsANameToo), JeremiGendron and Chirag Khatri (@ckhatri).

On the 30th January 2019, ARK Desktop Wallet version 2.1.1 was released. It improved the process of adding and running new ARK based blockchains within the wallet client. Other feature improvements implemented were:

- The ability to expand or collapse the wallet sidebar to see the full address and balance in the each wallet.
- An improved design for creating a new wallet address or importing an existing wallet.
- When broadcasting to multiple peers is activated, a loading screen appears after a transaction is signed and broadcast.

After numerous requests from the community, the Dynamic Fees feature was added to the ARK Mobile Wallet (v1.4.0) on the 8th February 2019. It became possible to send ARK and vote/register for an ARK delegate using the feature.

Other improvements to the functionality, user friendliness and appearance of both the desktop and mobile wallets were made (some requested by the community).

On the 11th February 2019, the mainnet ARK blockchain successfully switched to ARK Core v2.1 without affecting users. The codebase changed from JavaScript to TypeScript. Taking into account that TypeScript is a superset of JavaScript, the transition was easier than expected. One of the advantages of TypeScript is that it reports type and syntax errors at compile time, instead of runtime.

On the 20th February 2019, it became possible to buy, sell or store ARK on the Spend (https://www.spend.com) application. It automatically converts ARK to fiat currency in the background each time the Spend Visa Card is swiped or the mobile application is used. It permits users to spend ARK with over forty million merchants worldwide. It is available on Android and Apple mobile devices.

Since the beginning of the year, Justin Renken had been promoting the ARK Ecosystem by participating in interviews and speaking to intrigued audiences:

- On the 15th January 2019, he was a guest on the Smart Reach YouTube Channel (ITK Crypto #4) hosted by Tom White and Cryptoshi.
- On the 21st January 2019, he was interviewed on the Wild West Crypto Podcast Show (episode #44) hosted by Drew Taylor and L. Brent Bates.
- On the 29th January 2019, he spoke at DecentralizedSummit 2019.
- On the 9th March 2019, he attended the grand opening of the Crypto Blockchain Plug OTC in Los Angeles, California. He gave a presentation and handed out free ARK during a question and answer session. The venue later became the subject of the first episode of ARK.io Adventures on YouTube.

On the 11th March 2019, the second update to the ARK Core V2 codebase (v2.2) was released. It made the process of installing and managing ARK Core easier by integrating CLI (Command Line Interface). As a result, the external ARK Commander utility tool became deprecated. ARK Core had also become easier and quicker to install by making all of its plugins NPM (Node.js package manager) packages.

On the 14th March 2019, ARK Desktop Wallet version 2.3.0 was released. It improved the back-end of the client to increase performance and loading times. It also fixed code bugs and integrated new features including:

- Re-designed the delegate voting process to make it more user friendly
- The ability to sort wallet by name and balance via a filter menu
- The option to load a maximum number of wallet addresses from a connected Ledger hardware wallet
- Easy to see which delegates user is voting for, with each separate wallet, on wallets page when it's switched to list view.
- The ability to check a specific delegate wallet address in vote modal in the delegate tab.
- Reminds user to ignore or save changes in edit profile when leaving page
- Delegates can be sorted by rank, username, productivity or voting
- Display ticker price on dashboard, even when chart disabled.
- New, enhanced look and feel of the QR code scanner.

Since the previous desktop wallet release, nine developers had contributed to it by adding 13,337 and deleting 3,597 lines of code. As is customary, several Github contributors were notably applauded for their contribution. They were dated, vulet, kalgoop and danielstc).

On the 18th March 2019, the highly anticipated ARK Deployer V2 (compatible with the ARK Core V2 codebase) was released for simple and quick customer ARK based blockchain creation. The ARK Crew was quoted as saying:

> **"The ARK Deployer v2 provides the base for our upcoming graphical interface product (GUI version) that will allow for blockchain creation, as the slogan that we've been using for some time now suggests— *Point. Click. Blockchain."***

At this time, no official release date for the graphical user interface version of the ARK Deployer had been disclosed.

Whitepaper V2 Published

On the 4th April 2019, Michel Kraaijeveld joined the ARK Development Team as a frontend developer. He had been very active in the Github Development Bounty Program during which time he helped develop the ARK Desktop Wallet.

Following months of collaboration between members of the ARK Crew and the community, a new ARK Ecosystem Whitepaper (version 2.0.0) was published on the 5th April 2019. It brought together over two years of progress and achievement into an approximate 50 page and 15,000 words document. People interested in reading it can choose to skip familiar concepts and explore other content.

https://ark.io/Whitepaper.pdf

Besides helping the blockchain technology space to understand what the ARK Ecosystem is about, the whitepaper acts as an internal resource for the ARK Communications Team. It has been used as a solid resource to create material such as blog articles, videos and podcasts. Justin Renken subsequently read through the whitepaper on the ARK Crypto Podcast (episodes 33, 34 and 35).

"Once we get some of the initial commentary we'll also start to integrate images and other eye-candy touches we have prepped for better understanding and visualization of the data, and make it more appealing for print format."

At the time the whitepaper was published, the ARK Crew was eager to receive feedback from the community (see quote above).

On the 23rd April 2019, the mainnet ARK blockchain successfully switched to ARK Core V2.3. It streamlined the process of developing the codebase. It increased the VendorField from 64 to 255 bytes.

Other events which occurred during this period included:

- On the 22nd January 2019, the ARK Utilities tool was released. It is a library providing common functions for working with data.
- On the 15th February 2019, the Exodus Multi-Asset Wallet integrated ARK.
- On the 18th February 2019, ARK Core Docker was released. It is another tool for developers to quickly install and run an ARK node.
- On the 6th March 2019, the https://arkthoughts.com website went live thanks to generous donations from delegate jarunik. It is hosted by delegate deadlock.
- On the 22nd March 2019, ARK Desktop Wallet version 2.3.1 was released.
- On the 25th March 2019, ARK Desktop Wallet version 2.3.2 was released.

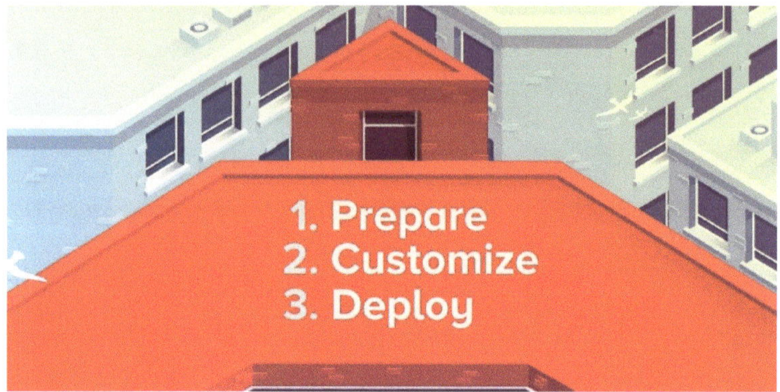

I. **ARK ECOSYSYEM BUSINESS OPERATIONS REFINED**

II. **ARK CREW ATTENDED CONSENSUS 2019 IN NEW YORK CITY**

III. **ARK DEPLOYER V2 (GUI) WENT LIVE ON 28TH MAY 2019**

IV. **SEVERAL ARK CORE, DESKTOP AND MOBILE UPDATES RELEASED**

V. **OFFICIAL ARK.IO WEBSITE REVAMPED ON 9TH JULY 2019**

9

ARK DEPLOYER GUI LAUNCHED

"With ARK Deployer and the documentation hub, more people than ever can now harness the power of the ARK Ecosystem and leverage the potential of blockchain technology."

Since its inception in early September 2016, the ARK Ecosystem had grown to become a more resilient, rigorously tested and respected blockchain technology project. Each member of the ARK Crew had worked hard to achieve set roadmap goals. Team expansion, especially during the summer of 2018, had increased the rate of code development during the last few months.

On the 7th May 2019, it was announced that ARK Ecosystem business operations had been refined to create a more structured environment for the team to take the project to the next level.

All three members of the Communications Team (Justin Renken, Carlye Wicklund and Sam Harper-Pittam) were applauded for their work in strengthening relationships with Github contributors, delegates and other ARK supporters. Justin Renken had recently been promoted to the position of Senior Brand Manager.

In addition to the Communications Team, the following roles were assigned. All positions below were well-deserved and clarified key points of contact to help increase the overall efficiency of the team:

- **Chairman:** Matthew D. Cox
- **Vice-Chairman**: Lars Rensing (re-elected)
- **Board Member**: Dr. Scott McPherson
- **President:** François-Xavier Thoorens
- **Vice-President:** Rok Černec (confirmed promotion on 1st May 2019)
- **Chief Technology Officer (CTO):** Kristjan Košič
- **Events & Integrations Manager**: Travis Walker
- **Finance & Compliance Manager:** Gerard Blezer
- **Lead Developer:** Brian Faust
- **Lead Designer**: Oleg Shcherbyna
- **Lead Network Infrastructure:** Velislav Valkov
- **ARK CORE**: Joshua Noack
- **ARK Desktop Wallet**: Alex Barnsley
- **ARK Mobile Wallet**: Lúcio Rubens
- **ARK Deployer**: Alex Barnsley
- **ARK Explorer**: Michel Kraaijeveld
- **ARK Internet-of-Things (IoT)**: Simon Downey
- **ARK Website**: Michel Kraaijeveld

In addition to the above, Kai Richards and Katie Phillips were hired as marketing managers within the newly formed marketing team. They are both from the United Kingdom.

From the 13th May to the 15th May 2019, one of the major conferences in the blockchain technology space called Consensus 2019 took place in New York City. It was a great opportunity for the ARK Ecosystem to showcase their achievements over the last twelve months, Over one hundred speakers and thousands of people attended the entire event.

Before Consensus 2019, four members of the ARK Crew (Matthew D. Cox, Travis Walker, Lars Rensing and Justin Renjen) attended a pre-conference event called the Magical Crypto Conference. It was held as an affordable alternative to Consensus 2019. The Magical Crypto Conference was created by Charlie Lee, Samson Mow, Riccard Spagni and WhalePanda.

On the 14th May 2019, Matthew D. Cox and Justin Renken, in that order, spoke on the Changelog Stage of Construct 2019 at Consensus 2019 about the following:

- Matthew D. Cox talked about the business side of the project. He covered material such as partnerships, ARK Crew hires and the status of the ARK Ecosystem finances.
- Justin Renken talked about the technology side of the project. He went through what the ARK Ecosystem had achieved so far and what they envisage to develop next.

Towards the end of Justin Renken's speech, he announced the release date of the ARK Deployer V2 GUI. The date 28th May 2019 was disclosed.

Other key highlights from Consensus 2019 were:

- François-Xavier Thoorens spoke with Andrew Munro from Crypto Finder.
- Justin Renken was interviewed by BLOCKTV, a live 24/7 online news channel dedicated to premium reporting on blockchain technology events.
- Travis Walker and Justin Renken made an appearance on the Bad Crypto Podcast to talk about the ARK Ecosystem and the new upcoming innovative ARK Deployer tool.

On the 21st May 2019, ARK Desktop Wallet version 2.4.0 was released. It was a major update and officially implemented the initial plugin system:

> **"It gives developers additional ways to expand the usability of the Desktop Wallet and develop innovative ways to interact with the ARK Ecosystem. Plugins are always optional for the user to install. Each plugin is installed on a per profile basis, allowing the ARK Desktop Wallet to remain free of any bloat. This means you get the experience you want, without any of the hassle you don't."**

The long term goal had been set to provide a fully featured "Plugin Marketplace' from which ARK users will be able to discover, investigate and install community developed plugins. It will also be possible to pay for certain premium plugins using the ARK cryptocurrency within the wallet client.

As the culmination of months of work hard, and as promised at Consensus 2019 in New York City, the new ARK Deployer was released on the 28th May 2019. It was described as a major milestone and a critical component of the ARK Ecosystem going forward. Justin Renken was quoted as saying:

> **"Today marks a major paradigm shift for ARK. ARK Deployer (alpha) is now live, giving everyone the power to create a customized blockchain in minutes using an intuitive graphical user interface. With ARK Deployer and the documentation hub, more people than ever can now harness the power of the ARK Ecosystem and leverage the potential of blockchain technology."**

It marked a pivotal moment by lowering the barrier to entry for any project, however small or large, wishing to leverage blockchain technology.

On the 12th June 2019, ARK Core version 2.4 was released for delegates to install, configure and monitor. It primarily switched the P2P communications layer from API to WebSockets. It changed the way in which ARK nodes interact with each other resulting in better performance and stronger resilience. Other aspects of the core codebase were also improved.

On the 26th June 2019, ARK Desktop Wallet version 2.5.0 was released. It improved support for Ledger Nano S and Nano X devices, enhanced the graphical user interface and integrated new features including:

- The ability to export wallets from the profile page.
- An option to hide the wallet button text.
- The ability to save sidebar sorting and filter settings.
- The addition of a status icon and plus/minus sign in transaction show modal
- An option to use the theme colour for the wallet filters instead of white.

Other events which occurred during May and June 2019 included:

- On the 9th May 2019, ARK Mobile Wallet version 1.4.2 was released.
- On the 17th May 2019, Travis Walker attended the first MLHacking and ARK Ecosystem workshop event.
- On the 4th June 2019, ARK CEO François-Xavier Thoorens appeared in the French press for *Les Échos*, the first daily French financial newspaper.
- On the 12th June 2019, the ARK/BTC trading pair went live on the DOBI cryptocurrency exchange platform.
- On the 12th June 2019, ARK Desktop Wallet version 2.4.1 was released.
- On the 14th June 2019, ARK Mobile Wallet version 1.4.4 was released. It had been updated to become ARK Core version 2.4 compatible.
- On the 20th June 2019, it became possible for people to purchase ARK tokens using credit cards and bank transfers at https://crypto.com.

After collaboration across all departments of the ARK Crew, a revamped official ARK Ecosystem website (announced on the 27th June 2019) went live on the 9th July 2019. All pages had been optimally formatted to increase engagement, accessibility to resources and create an overall better user friendly website. Ultimately, its design had been streamlined to be more simple, clean and easier to navigate.

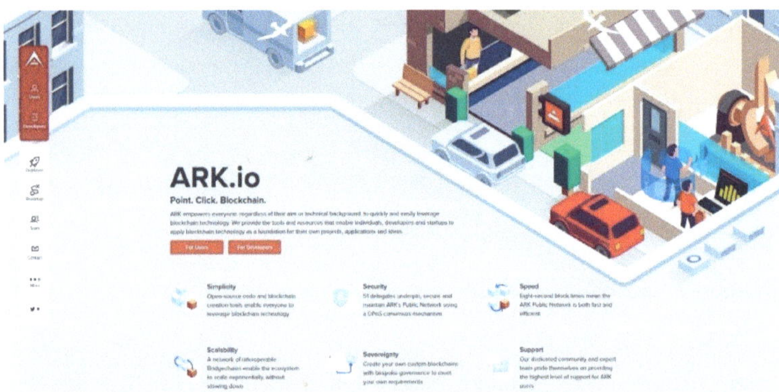

"ARK empowers everyone, regardless of their aim or technical background, to quickly and easily leverage blockchain technology. We provide the tools and resources that enable individuals, developers and startups to apply blockchain technology as a foundation for their own projects, applications and ideas."

It had also been re-designed to tailor for multiple audiences depending on what content they are seeking to investigate. To be specific, two separate hubs are accessible directly from the official ARK Ecosystem website:

- **User Hub**—for users to discover how they can utilise the ARK Ecosystem to their benefit (secure funds, share ideas, spend ARK etc.).
- **Developer Hub**—for developers to discover how they can contribute to the open source project (build, contribute and earn ARK etc.).

www.ingramcontent.com/pod-product-compliance
Lightning Source LLC
Chambersburg PA
CBHW041155050326
40690CB00004B/565

9781699908884